Practical Solutions for Overcoming Obstacles

As a Working Parent

Alexandria Fields MSW, LISW-S

Copyright © 2022 Alexandria Fields

All rights reserved.

ISBN: 978-1-7366554-2-9

DEDICATION

This book is dedicated to my fellow working parents who are doing their best to hold down the fort at home and show up to work each day with not-so-hidden bags under their eyes and totally hidden cheerios stuck to their butt.

CONTENTS

Chapter	Title	Page
	Introduction	2
1	Who Do You Want to Become?	3
2	Who Do You Want Your Kids to Become?	29
3	Why is Avoidance So Tempting?	46
4	Dealing with Emotions	58
5	Self-Worth, Self-Love, and Self-confidence	76
6	Where Am I Going Wrong?	97
7	Tools for Success	111
8	Making The Change You Deserve	125
9	Don't Let it Go, Let It Be	137
10	The Elephant in The Room	148
11	Final Thoughts	164
	References	166

Introduction

The title of this book might feel misleading as you read through the chapters. Practical Solutions for Overcoming Obstacles as a Working Parent is not a book of life hacks for maximizing your schedule, improving your ability to multitask, or shame you into being more present when playing with your kids (those parenting books already exist)! This book seeks to go deeper and help you to improve your functioning as an adult and will show you how changing your habits can elevate your parenting through leading by example. I will undoubtedly use some parenting-guilt by showing you how the changes I suggest will also benefit your child(ren). I hope you can read this book with an open mind and consider implementing the ideas slowly and steadily. This is not a book that I recommend you binge-read in one week/month; rather, I encourage you to read and mark up one chapter at a time – reread as necessary (I have a feeling you might experience some interruptions along the way), and journal to process your thoughts. You will find journal prompts within and at the end of each chapter. This would be a great book for a parenting group to process together or one that you can share insights you have had with your friends over coffee. Reading a book is great; living in a healthier way because of reading a book is better.

1 WHO DO YOU WANT TO BECOME?

"You are never too old to set another goal or to dream a new dream." — C. S. Lewis

- How do you want your child(ren) to describe you when they are older?
- Who do you want to be after the kids fly the nest?
- Who did you enjoy being prior to having kids?

Many parents get so wrapped up in their identity as a parent, that they completely lose sight of who they were (and are) independent of their children. Their identities get completely wrapped up in their kids' lives (dance mom, PTO volunteer, Scout leader, soccer coach, chauffer, etc.) Without a well-defined identity, you are likely to drift from one event to another, one soccer practice to another, one school awards banquet to another, etc. until one day your child goes to college, and you have completely lost your way. That can be a painful time for any parent; however, it is amplified when you are lacking friendships, hobbies and/or interests outside of your role as a parent. Having those relationships and hobbies will serve as your stabilizing coping skills. I know many of you enjoy being identified primarily as a parent, it is a noble identity! I am here to push you into new ways of thinking, new ways that remind you of your worth as it stretches far beyond that of being a mom or a dad. Your children will also benefit from this growth as they will learn a template for living that allows them to remain open to new experiences and allows them to avoid falling into the pressures associated with fixating on only one role.

A few years ago, someone asked me how I thought my kids would describe me when they were older. Gulp. That was a hard question to answer! I generally think I am a good mom: fun and loving, patient yet firm and nurturing, playful and structured simultaneously; however, when my kids misbehave or break significant rules, I can be more authoritative in nature. I have been known to yell. I am quicker to use time-out than I would like to admit. I wonder which way they will remember me. Would they report to others the ten good memories or the one bad memory? This is a rabbit hole I could see as extremely dangerous for most parents. A second thought I had that prompted further panic was. "*What would they tell their therapist about me when they are young adults*". It is always the mom's fault, right?! Instead of falling into this rabbit hole and beating yourself up, I encourage you to use the questions as motivation for change. Every person, parents included, has room for growth. You might need to grow by being more playful, perhaps you would like to spend more time together at the dinner table, maybe you need to decrease the yelling. Shaming yourself will not achieve the results you want; if it worked, I am sure we would all be perfect by now!

Instead of getting lost in my own panic, I chose to get busy. I needed to solve this problem that I had created in my mind. I discovered that the questions posed above are one portion of the equation needed for a parent to define their long-term goals. The easy answer that comes to mind for many is "I want my kids to like me". That is a faulty and short-sighted view of which I implore you to discard. Treat that thought as if it were poison ivy and back away! You have the ability and the right to dream bigger than that, I intend to guide you toward the self-esteem needed to be a better parent and expect more for your children's future.

I invite you to start this book off with intention and purpose. Do not skip this part and say "*I will get to it later*" because that rarely happens. Take some time now, before moving to the next segment, to reflect on the questions posed at the beginning of the chapter:

- How do you want your child(ren) to describe you when they are older?
- Who do you want to be after the kids fly the nest?
- Who did you enjoy being prior to having kids?

_____
_____
_____
_____
_____
_____
_____
_____
_____
_____
_____
_____
_____
_____
_____
_____
_____
_____
_____
_____
_____
_____
_____
_____
_____
_____
_____
_____

Understanding your style

Understanding your parenting style and giving it a name can help reduce judgments you have. Each style has pros and cons (and most parents are a blend of several styles). In describing the styles below, I urge you to credit yourself for the positive attributes and not panic about the risks. Learning the risks can open your eyes and empower you to make minor changes to improve your functioning. There many parenting types that can be defined and there are no shortage of books and blogs on the topic. All parenting types have strong opportunities and obstacles that can lead to positive or detrimental outcomes. I want to take a moment to look at the basic risks and rewards below so that you can see why change might benefit your family.

For simplicity's sake I will define five primary types, please note that you may be a combination of them.

1. The friend
2. The ruler
3. The obsessive
4. The worried
5. The assured

The Friend

The friend is preoccupied with keeping their child happy and doing anything in their power to ensure their child has fun and is happy. This parent wants the child to brag to their peers about how cool the parent is. They struggle with the notion of enforcing limits and never want to be the authority figure. This parent is generally well liked by the child and child's friends and as such, playdates and sleepovers are likely to occur in their home. This can allow you the benefit of keeping a close eye on your child and rest confidently in the knowledge that they are safe. A risk of this parenting type is the increased likelihood of enmeshment between the "friend parent" and the child. Often the parent leans too much on the child to be their confidant and problem solver which is too large of a responsibility for a child (regardless of their age). The child is likely to experience anxiety as they try to process the parents' problems. Children and teens do not have a fully developed sense of self or impulse control which leads to this child often developing a sense of entitlement and struggling to hear "no" from all people in their lives. This parent is often lost and does not know what to do when the child misbehaves which leads to their blaming of others and joining the child in playing the victim role (such as "my teacher is out to get me".)

The Ruler

The "ruler" is queen or king of their castle. This parent is an authoritarian, a take-no-nonsense parent. Their kids often lie or hide their mistakes because they fear the consequences of any infraction. This parent is high on expectations and low on warmth. The child is not given many choices in their own life because the parent does not trust that the child can do well or make wise choices on their own. The ruler also fears being embarrassed by the child's choices. Ruler parents are quick to use shaming statements and corporal punishment to deal with infractions, thus leading to avoidance and resentment from the child. These kids are usually very well behaved, especially in public, and are high achievers; however, struggle with low self-esteem, depression, and anxiety. They learn not to trust themselves and fear disappointing people in their lives (whether real or perceived.)

The Obsessive

The obsessive parent is overwhelmed with appearances and how others perceive their family. He/She will want to adopt a Martha Stewart personality when it comes to hosting dinners, volunteering in their kids' classroom, being active in the community and ensuring their lawn is meticulously landscaped. The obsessive parent can present as a perfectionist and is likely to appear deceptively more in control than they feel, meaning that people are unlikely to offer help because they seem to have it all under control. They have a difficult time asking for help and struggle to connect with their children because of the unattainable expectations they have of everyone in their life (including themselves). They are likely to be obsessive and micromanage the child's performance, wanting to assure the desired outcome, even if that means strong-arming coaches and teachers. Children who grow up in this environment can be grateful for everything they have and can also struggle to feel that they will ever be good enough. They can build resentment toward the high expectations and thus "give up" as they don't feel they can live up to the expectation. It is a common parenting style for parents who were naturally high achievers and now they are parenting a child who struggles academically and is also common with working parents who are trying to "do it all".

The Worried

The worried parent is a ball of anxiety. They worry about things that are unlikely to happen, even ten-twenty years into the future. They may hover over the child at the playground and feel obligated to chaperone all field trips to ensure there is no distress being experienced by their child. Their child might define them as a "nagger" or "always on my case" because this parent is always reminding the child about chores, expectations, safety, and the future. This child tends to become quite anxious themselves because there are given the message from childhood that the world is unsafe, that the child is incapable of keeping themselves safe, and that they cannot succeed without rigid structure. This parent is hypervigilant to all sorts of threats (real and imagined); due to the precautions that they take, the child often does not learn how to problem solve on their own. Sometimes this child will feel more loved and cared for than other children due to their parent's constant presence; however, enmeshment needs to be avoided for both parties to develop healthy identities.

The Assured

The assured parent has confidence and owns a level of acceptance about life circumstances that allows the child to grow into a confident adult. The assured parent knows that bumps and bruises will happen, knows that their child is capable of overcoming aversity, and pushes their child to make empowered decisions (even if they are not the best choices)! They are unlikely to be embarrassed buy their child's fashion choices or desires to express themselves as they grow. This parent also cultivates their own identity outside of their children and does not wreck themselves with guilt for using a babysitter or daycare to get their own needs met. That is not to say this parent is negligent because an assured parent is also engaged and attuned to their child's needs and can easily tell friends and work "no" to be present for the family. The goal of this book is to teach and empower you to be an assured parent, even if you keep aspects of your natural parenting style (whichever it may be).

All parents will likely see themselves in each subtype described above to some degree and that is okay! It is important that you take an honest inventory of your patterns and work toward becoming a more assured parent over time. As I stated, it is the overarching goal of this book: to teach you the value and benefits of increasing your own confidence, both in your child's and your own ability to overcome difficulties and grow into the healthiest versions of yourselves. I have no doubt that you want your child(ren) to grow into a confident and capable young adult, the reality is that starting in toddlerhood, you can help them with this by helping yourself! When they are young, you can take steps toward helping them develop a strong sense of self, the ability to problem-solve, and how to cope with their emotions. I will be transparent here and remind you that to achieve those goals for your child, you must first achieve them for yourself and as such, this book focuses more on you than on your parenting. If you want your child to use favorable adjectives to describe their childhood, applying the strategies in this book will help! The children of assured parents are more likely to feel loved, empowered, confident, and have higher self-esteem.

In what ways do you see yourself in each of the five parenting styles? Which parenting-style habits do you want to decrease, and which do you want to increase?

The question from the beginning of the chapter lingers; who did you enjoy being prior to having kids? Did you have a hobby? Did you attend clubs/groups/sports/meetings prior to having children? Did you see friends with regularity? Being a new parent can throw your personal life into a tailspin! I would like for you to take some time to level the plane so that we can get back on course. Being a parent is one component of your identity. Being a parent is not your only identity.

Many of the problems we are going to explore in this book are a direct result of having an unstable identity. What I have found as a therapist, is that the clients who do not get better, don't know who they are! What I mean by that is that they have not developed their identity by joining groups/clubs or growing a hobby. This is often due to social anxiety, which is real and can require a professional to help you work through it. People who stay depressed are usually not part of any sort of community that helps define their values and morals. Have you heard the adage that "if you don't stand for something, you'll fall for anything"? Never fear, none of us have it truly figured out, I am not asking you to commit to one singular hobby or group and stick with it forever! The best thing we can do is to make choices along the way that help us feel more competent and self-respecting.

First, you must evaluate what things you enjoy in life! What is fun to one person in life does not always equate to fun for another. Our first task is to identify interests that you are (or want to be) involved with and that are (or you think they could be) fun to you. The choices need to be realistic (i.e.: for your regional climate, the time of year, your financial situation, etc.) and could be available without much delay. It is also important that you throw yourself into enjoying the activity to give it a fair chance! We are exceptionally good at worrying... about whether we deserve it, what else we should be doing with our time, whether we can afford it, if we look silly and are being judged, etc. To reap the benefits, we need to give our brains a break and really allow ourselves to mindfully enjoy the experience!

Consider the following hobbies, interests, and activities and <u>circle</u> (if you haven't noticed, we are going to mark this book up!) the ones you might be interested in. This is not time for you to talk yourself out of it, research it, or make any decisions, just go with your gut!

- Book club

- Hiking
- Writing
- Baking/cooking
- Playing musical instrument
- Bible study
- Painting
- Running/jogging
- Singing
- Teaching
- Crafting
- Sewing
- Exercise
- Swimming/diving
- Volunteering
- Fishing
- Camping
- Acting/Improv
- Woodworking
- Meditation
- Community activism
- Photography
- Rock Climbing
- Blogging
- Crafting
- Board games
- Other:

Taking steps toward having hobbies and increasing the adult fun in your life can help you to build up a coat of armor against the stresses that will inevitably happen throughout your days and weeks. Have you ever noticed how much more emotional you are when you are physically ill or in pain? The same irritability starts to creep up when you go long periods of time without socializing, engaging in hobbies and/or having fun! As a parent, this may seem like a natural progression because you continually give up your plans and put your desires in the back seat to prioritize what your children/families request of you. If you do not make time (yes, schedule it), it is unlikely to happen, which will result in your moods dipping slowly and steadily over time. Depression and irritability will slowly creep up on you and before you know it, you are not an incredibly fun person to be around.

To feel confident as a parent, you will need to be confident as a person (remember – you are more than your parent identity). Having a hobby and friends outside of your circle of other parents is one step toward a well-rounded identity. This means that you may find enjoyment in having one hobby on your own, one with your spouse/partner and one with a friend. None of the activities you partake in needs to be all encompassing or obsessive; I want you to look for casual enjoyment, a hobby you can turn to over the next 18– years!

Values based living

In conjunction with building your confidence through curating "you time" of hobbies and interests, it is critical that you align at least one hobby or activity with your values. Values-based living is a sure-fire way to build your coat of armor against depression. In my work as a therapist, I am consistently reminded of the need for all people to find, develop, and have values-based passions in your life. Values-based living means that you have a strong sense of the actions, thoughts, and morals that you hold at a high standard, and you make choices that align with them. You make choices that:

- Increase your self-esteem.
- Leave you feeling like you can hold your head high
- Cause you to feel fulfilled.
- Give you a feeling of purpose.
- Allow you to feel connected to others.

For your mental health and the wellness of your relationships, the need for values-based living and values-based parenting is amplified! Your children can be and are a passion of yours; however, as you have read, you need to have a life outside of them. This will help them develop independence and a healthy view of relationships as they grow into young adults. This list of values is not comprehensive; however, it is a place you can start and use as a jumping off point. I want you to slowly read through the list and check off the ones that seem important to you. If you are not sure what they mean, take a moment to look them up and then write a helpful synonym next to it for your own reference.

- Authenticity
- Achievement
- Adventure
- Altruism
- Authority
- Balance
- Beauty
- Belonging
- Boldness
- Compassion
- Challenge
- Community
- Contribution
- Creativity
- Curiosity
- Determination
- Enjoyment
- Excitement
- Fairness
- Faith
- Happiness
- Honesty
- Humor
- Independence
- Influence
- Inner Harmony
- Integrity
- Justice
- Kindness
- Knowledge
- Leading by Example
- Learning
- Love
- Loyalty
- Meaningful Work
- Optimism
- Peace
- Personal Growth
- Pleasure
- Popularity
- Recognition
- Reputation
- Respect
- Responsibility
- Security
- Self-Respect
- Service Work
- Spirituality
- Stability
- Success
- Status
- Trustworthiness
- Wealth
- Wisdom
- Other: _____

This list of values can assist you in moving through the rest of the chapter. I now want you to re-read the list of what you checked off, slowly, and highlight the ones that seem most important to you. This may be 1-3 values, or it may be 10-15. Take a moment to see if any of them can be combined into a category that appeals to you and jot that down where it says "other". From there, cross-reference your values against your chosen hobbies from earlier in this chapter. Do you see any that make sense together? For example, if you chose the activity of volunteering and the values of meaningful work and responsibility, you could reflect on how powerful it will be for your identity to begin volunteer work. I want you to use that as motivation to make plans to take action.

In reviewing my hobbies and values, these are areas I could put more effort into as a way to grow my identity:

_____
_____
_____
_____
_____
_____
_____
_____
_____
_____

I mentioned above the need for your hobby to be realistic. Season may play a role in your interests as well. Consider this example: one of my winter passions is quilting/sewing. I very much enjoy the process of finding a pattern, seeking the perfect fabric, and putting the product together. It becomes quite therapeutic for me, a mindful escape into my creative nature. This may seem like an antiquated hobby; however, I liken it to carpenters building furniture. The resulting quilt or garments are incredibly rewarding. This hobby tends to take a complete backseat in my life one the weather breaks in the spring. When the weather is more comfortable for me, I am far more likely to be hiking or gardening outdoors and have little desire to sit inside and sew!

What I want you to find is an activity that provides you with the sensation of lost time (meaning you can get mindfully engrossed in the task and loose sense of time) and feelings of pride, joy, accomplishment, and serenity. This experience of mindfulness will highlight the power of values-based living. The things you are passionate about will leave you feeling full and motivated as opposed to lazy and worthless. For many a contrast would be how they feel after watching television. A common report after screen time across ages, genders and socioeconomic status groups are feelings of fatigue and regret paired with the loss of motivation and productivity. Those are not feelings I want you to have!

To define a long-term goal that will sustain your interest, I recommend finding one that speaks to your core values. Taking steps towards values-based living and having fun that lines up with your core values will build your confidence, self-worth, and self-esteem (as a human and as a parent) while providing you with a huge leap away from depression, low self-worth, and lack of identity. Living according to your values will also help you feel insulated and protected from negative events and stresses that seem to happen inevitably. In addition to creating fun in your day-to-day life, I also urge you to take steps toward a longer-term set of goals. Focusing on the long-term takes a little more effort to plan.

The act of values-based living is also an activity that can be done with the whole family. This is something I put into practice for myself and my family. My family has identified our five core values: adventure, teamwork, integrity, perseverance, and respect. We posted them up in our dining room. When making major (and minor) choices, I try to be sure the decision aligns with at least one of our values. As a result of this, we are more likely to encourage our kids to keep trying, even when their homework is difficult, we sit down and discuss what respect and integrity mean (it is never too early to start the conversation) so that they are empowered to be respectful of one another and of their peers/authority figures at school, we share examples of where they do and can show integrity, and when we have a down day, we are more likely to go exploring at a new park than sit in front of the television!

These are some values that my family can agree upon:

_____
_____
_____
_____
_____
_____

We can put them into practice by:

_____
_____
_____
_____
_____
_____
_____
_____
_____
_____
_____
_____
_____
_____
_____
_____
_____
_____
_____
_____
_____
_____
_____
_____
_____
_____

After you identify your core values and ideal hobbies, if you find it difficult to turn them into action, I can share with you a step-by-step guide to use! If you identify a value and do not take steps toward living it, you might feel worse as it can highlight a gap in your ideal vs real lives. It will be helpful to take steps toward breaking one identified value down into goals, smaller steps, and even smaller baby steps! Do not try to tackle all the values you chose at once, that would be too overwhelming. It is also too overwhelming to try to tackle a value without breaking it down (Afterall, if it were that easy wouldn't we all do it already?) Here is a outline you follow:

Step One: Pick one of the values to work on first (this does not mean the others are not important).

_____
_____
_____
_____
_____
_____

Step Two: Identify some goals associated with the value.

_____
_____
_____
_____
_____
_____

Step Three: Pick one of the goals (this does not mean the others are not important).

_____
_____
_____
_____
_____
_____

Step Four: Identify some steps needed to work toward that goal. What are the things that stop you from tackling it? Problem solving these can help you identify the steps.

_____
_____
_____
_____
_____

Step Five: Pick one step to work on now (this does not mean the others are not important).

_____
_____
_____
_____
_____

Step Six: Identify any baby steps that might be needed to work toward that first step.

_____
_____
_____
_____
_____

Step Seven: Pick ONE action to take THIS WEEK!

_____
_____
_____
_____
_____

It is important that you take action quickly to get the ball rolling. Remember from science that an object in motion stays in motion while an object at rest stays at rest. This is true for human behavior also! You can start this book off right, chapter one…challenge one!

Finding the Time

In a TED talk by Laura Vandercam in 2017 on time management, she gets real and does the math for us:

"There are 168 hours in a week. Twenty-four times seven is 168 hours. That is a lot of time. If you are working a full-time job, so 40 hours a week, sleeping eight hours a night, so 56 hours a week-- that leaves 72 hours for other things. That is a lot of time. You say you are working 50 hours a week, maybe a main job and a side hustle. Well, that leaves 62 hours for other things. You say you are working 60 hours. Well, that leaves 52 hours for other things …"

I want you to pause and reflect on the fact that you have a choice in how you spend your time. I think most people tend to feel obligated to do certain things: work, attend family functions, keep up with the news, put our kids in eight activities at any given time but we do not often stop to evaluate the reality of our choice in the matter. Our discussions are peppered with "I *have* to….." Instead of "I *choose* to…". We fail to accept that we spend our time doing what choose to make time for. We make time for what we believe is important– that can either mean what we value, or it can mean what we feel is expected of us. I propose that you take a both/and approach, rather than an either/or approach.

One example I can share is that going to work and being a diligently hard worker is a value of mine. Spending time with my family is also a value of mine. I prioritize them both; it is not an either/or. Sometimes this means I take a day off to spend time with my family. Sometimes it means that I take my kids to work with me. Sometimes it means I work long hours with intense focus. There is no right answer; however, there is an answer that supports your values and leaves you with less regret. You will need to evaluate your values and find similar both/and solutions in order to achieve the values-based living that I suggest.

That same TED Talk Laura Vandercam did a time study of over 1000 very busy women with a variety of roles to play (business owners, moms, caregivers of aging parents, active in community organizations, etc.). During her study, one woman had a home plumbing crisis that resulted in sever hours of clean up and work above and beyond her meticulously scheduled life. We have time for what we make time for.

She also found a mom of six who owned a small business that actively took time out for morning hikes because she takes this concept to heart. Both are successful. Both are good moms.

Another way I have used to confront my own denial of this issue is by checking how much time I am spending on various apps. You can check this by downloading apps that track it for you or, some phones have that feature built in. Realizing that we "waste time" can be a reminder that we could make time for hobbies and interests if we wanted to.

Are you willing to admit that you make time for what you want to make time for?

_____
_____
_____
_____
_____
_____
_____
_____
_____
_____
_____
_____
_____

Parent Guilt

I am already aware that your biggest barrier, aside from finding time and energy for your own hobbies, is your parent guilt. Parent guilt is a topic that deserves a book of its own; but for now, I will address it here. Parent guilt is the overwhelming sense or feeling that you have done something terribly wrong and usually selfish, which you believe will result in long term damage to your child(ren). Parent guilt is cruel and relentless. It is usually the strongest when you are taking time for yourself (and thus your brain will highlight the fact that you are taking time away from them) and at night. Parent guilt comes from the belief that as a parent, you must put the needs of your child in front of your own, 100% of the time.

Parent guilt sounds like:
- "Do I play with them enough?"
- "Do they know how much I love them?"
- "Am I failing as a parent?"
- "Do I scold them too much?"
- "Are they ok?"
- "Are they crying because I left?"
- "What if my schedule is the reason they have to miss something?"
- "I waited so long to have kids; I don't want to miss any time with them"

What are some of the things you tell yourself when parent guilt is high?
_____
_____
_____
_____
_____
_____

    It is critical that you recognize the guilty thought and remind yourself that you do not have to accept the narrative it presents as fact. You must remind yourself that <u>doing what is right for your mental health and your identity teaches your child(ren) to do the same as they age.</u> I challenge you to accept the belief that by prioritizing your own needs, you are also prioritizing their needs. They will need to learn healthy detachment and trust that you will return. They will need to learn that you are coming back and that while you are gone, they can still have fun and be confident in your love for them. Your absences can teach them to listen to their gut and develop their own sense of self. Parental guilt is a bully that will try to keep you from attending to your own needs and desires.

    Parent guilt can even peak up when you run an errand alone and can show up as spouse guilt (in which you also feel like you are failing as a spouse by asking them to be the primary parent while you engage in your activity). You are allowed to have needs and parents tend to live by a myth that their needs are no longer important once they have a child. Your needs are not only important, but you also need to direct resources (such as time, energy, and money) toward your needs.

Coping with parent guilt requires you to recognize what guilt is. Guilt is a message that you have done something that violates your own personal values. If unchecked, it will continue to grow. According to Dialectical Behavioral Therapy, it is important that we evaluate if an emotion is justified or not, prior to moving forward. In the circumstance I am describing you are a parent who parents with love and affection, you meet their needs (physical, emotional, spiritual, etc.), and you are present with them more often than not and you decide to join a weekly activity that aligns with your values. In that scenario, guilt is not justified because you have not done something egregious. If the emotion is not justified, the treatment is called "opposite action". That means that you act opposite to your emotional urge until the intensity decreases enough that you can notice. The urge with parent guilt is generally to cancel your plans and give more time and attention to your children instead of funneling it to your own needs. Opposite action needs you to do what makes you feel guilty, over and over again, while making it public to people who will not reject you. This might mean that you post about the hobby/activity to social media and invite friends to go with you. It might mean you discuss it in therapy. However, when you face it, be sure to face it with confident body posture and calm, encouraging self-talk.

Scheduling Barriers

With three children of my own, I understand the complexities involved with scheduling all too well. My children have gone to three different schools/programs for several consecutive years while my husband and I both worked full time. Our life seemed to be a never-ending cycle of pick-ups and drop-offs, sprinkled with miniature panic moments over fear that I would forget one of them at practice or school! Scheduling woes are real. Problem solving them takes time, creativity, and a willingness to try new things. If your children are younger than school age, it also involves a lot of money as daycare is not cheap!

I hope that in reading this chapter thus far, you have started to come to the realization that your needs are important and are worth a cost to both your budget, your comfort zone, and your family's time. I recognize that some of the ideas below will cause you to immediately say *"no way, I cannot do that, that's not available in my area, etc."*; however, I challenge you to explore these options with an open mind.

- Drop-in daycare.
- Swap childcare at no cost with a friend/neighbor/family member.
- Split your kids up between different friends/family members/neighbors to make the job easier.
- Tag-team with partner and schedule your groups/hobbies on different nights, celebrate the 1:1 time that you will each get with your child(ren) and the 1:1 time you will have with yourself.
- Babysitter services in your city.
- Hire a local high school or college student.
- Find a gym that has childcare.
- Schedule a hangout with other moms and allow children to play while grown-ups attend to their own activity.
- Schedule your events for after bedtime or before waking hours.
- Explore after school childcare options at your child's school before or after the school day.
- Schedule your events to occur during your child's activities.
- Other: _____

Questions to Journal on:

1. What parenting style jumped out at you, is this the one you want your kids to describe you as?
2. What stops you from seeking out and starting a hobby?
3. Who could watch your kids while you engage in a new (or resume an old) venture?
4. What activities do you engage in that leave you feeling worse, what times of day do these tend to happen?
5. How do you feel when considering the idea of having hobbies

and taking steps toward living in alignment with your long-term goals? How will you cope with parent guilt that arises?

2 WHO DO YOU WANT YOUR KIDS TO BECOME?

"Children do learn what they live. Then they grow up to live what they've learned" — Dorothy Nolte

Your Habits

In the last chapter, we looked at your identity and who you would like to be; now, we need to look at your child(ren) and who you hope they will become! As you know, the wellbeing of your children is generally something you will put above your own (to a fault) and I fully intend to manipulate that fact and use it to motivate you.

I do not think I have ever met someone who wanted their child to fail in life. I also do not think I have ever met someone who did not have hopes and dreams for their child's future. Those hopes and dreams generally includes things about the child finding fulfillment, passion, and financial comfort in their career, having a secure group of friends with diverse interests, and keeping their mind and body healthy. Those are AMAZING goals for any human to strive for. The goals certainly paint the picture of a fulfilled and successful adult. While I know that each generation wants more for their child, the lofty image I painted of your child's future begs one question:

Are you living up to those expectations in a way that provides them an example to follow?

_____
_____
_____
_____

Take a moment to go back and re-read the quote at the start of this chapter. How are they supposed to know what to do if you do not show them in your own actions? In this chapter, I am not tackling things as intense as childhood trauma, neglect, parental addiction, or domestic violence; those are topics for other books. I am referring to your daily actions, smaller choices, and little habits that they see and learn from. You may have heard expressions that remind you that little ears are always listening, and little eyes are always watching right? Did you ever stop and think what sorts of things your kids are seeing and hearing (from you)? I would venture to guess that for many of us, we have more "bad habits" than we would like to admit, check off the ones that you know you do (at least more than you should) and circle the ones that you know you do too much:

- Texting and driving
- Eye rolling
- Gossiping
- Judging others (making comments about neighbors, co-workers, family members, friends, etc.)
- Road rage
- Not keeping healthy bedtime
- Cursing
- Phone addiction
- Television addiction
- Nightly wine/beer to unwind
- Impulse buying
- Responding to work emails at all hours
- Vaping or smoking
- Complaining
- Not engaging in play
- Avoidance of exercise
- Using sugar/candy as a justified reward for a bad day
- Daily caffeine use
- Toxic positivity (more on this below)

If you look through this list, I imagine that it does not align with the type of teen or young adult that you would like to your little one to grow into. The behaviors listed above are likely to sabotage any person's attempt to feel contentment, have healthy friendships and maintain a healthy mind and body. It might not be "fair" to be forced to "lead by example"; and yet, I wonder what the outcomes would be for yourself and your little ones if you were the parent who prioritized:

- Exercise
- Taking evening walks
- Sketching or coloring in a coloring book
- Meditation
- Drinking water more than any other beverage
- Reading
- Journaling
- Bedtime routines
- Being present in conversations
- Giving people the benefit of the doubt
- Embracing diversity and different cultures
- Ongoing adult education

Which of the above are you most willing to consider implementing and practicing in your daily life, why?

_____
_____
_____
_____
_____
_____
_____
_____
_____
_____
_____
_____
_____
_____

In addition to setting a good example for your kids, I imagine that if you embraced and prioritized healthier habits, you would be less stressed and irritable, less angry, less resentful, your physical health would improve, you would attract healthy relationships and your children would want to be around you! As teens, they might even brag about you (maybe...)!

Since we all agree that they are always watching you (case in point...that time your little one repeated something you did not want them to repeat...) it is imperative that you are engaging in behaviors that you want them to emulate! I realize that changing your actions can be difficult and may seem overwhelming. At times it may seem too difficult to maintain the motivation necessary to change your bad habits for the long-haul. This is especially true when the bad habit is seen as "normal" for your culture (such as gossip, binge-watching shows, or drinking every night). In this next section we will look at how to change actions, behaviors, and habits.

In what ways would your life improve if you decreased the unhealthy habits and increased the healthy habits suggested by the lists on the previous pages?

_____
_____
_____
_____
_____
_____
_____
_____
_____
_____
_____
_____
_____
_____
_____
_____
_____
_____
_____
_____
_____
_____
_____

Thoughts, Feelings, Actions

Our own habits are perpetuated by our thoughts, feelings, and actions. You probably know that your thoughts, your feelings, and your actions are all connected, but you may not know that the relationship is transactional. A transactional relationship means that while one of the three (thoughts, feelings, actions) influences another of the three, that change will in turn influence another factor. None of the three can exist without the other two. Any change will cause more change, and in that regard, it does not matter where you start…or does it? This begs the question, where do we make the change in our lives if we want to think differently, act differently, or feel differently? Do you change the thoughts you have; do you change your actions? If you change your actions, is that before or after the thoughts? Do you change how you feel about the situation? The easy answer is change in any of the three areas will provoke change in the other two; however, I will tell you that I believe that it is easier to change your actions first. When we start acting/behaving differently, I believe you will notice thinking differently much quicker than if you wait until you feel motivated.

Think about it through the lens of this example: You wake up to your alarm. You are very tired as you did not sleep well. Your child was up late crying, emotional about something that had happened. Is it easier to improve your mood by laying there and forcing yourself to think *"gee, I am so glad to be awake early! The fact that my body feels heavy, and my mind feels cloudy is no problem! I look forward to seeing people today who may ask me how I'm doing!*" OR is it easier to improve your mood by getting out of bed and getting a shower while listening to some upbeat music? I imagine that if you try to wait until you change your thoughts, you may end up staying in bed for the entire day! I would never say that jumping out of bed is easy; but, if you are able to change your behavior, you may feel pride, competence, and contentment.

I know that acting differently than you may feel it is one of the hardest things to do. Think back to the last time you were feeling depressed, I bet it would have been nearly impossible to get you to go for a jog! The last time you were experiencing intense anxiety, it probably would have been quite a challenge to convince you to go lay down and listen to a meditation. And the last time you were fuming mad, I would think it would have been difficult to motivate you to go for a walk…and yet this is what I suggest! Why would I suggest something so radically difficult? Mainly because if you do, you will see how quickly it remedies the intensity of the emotion and thoughts. Furthermore, I propose that if you do it a few times in a row, you will begin to trust the process…this is pretty much what all people with good habits say about how they stick to their routines! Over time, you will learn that your intuition can be trusted.

What are some habits that you want to increase but struggle to find the motivation for?

_____
_____
_____
_____
_____
_____

Research

As a parent, you have the added motivation of knowing that your kids are watching and learning from your actions. If parent guilt alone were successful at getting us to change, we would all be the image of physical and mental health! I do not think intelligence is the issue. You know what and why you should change, and yet you don't do it. Why don't you make these changes despite (sometimes YEARS of) intending to? How do you make changes when you feel stuck and immobilized by your anxieties? My simple answer for you is: research.

I have found over the years that one must build up the wind that will blow their own sails, rather than waiting for the conditions to be perfect for steering their vessel. Researching helps us to remember why the change (and required effort) is a good idea each time our procrastination or resistance to change rears its ugly head. Change takes time and you might notice that you get stuck in the step of contemplation (thinking about changing), not sure how to get to action. I see research as a way to build a bridge, or lay stepping-stones for yourself. I recommend that you do not wait for other people to motivate you, using research, you can motivate yourself. You cannot wait for motivation to magically wash over you. You must fuel your own motivation by learning as much as you can about what you want to do and why! Research is a *behavior,* which I showed you is an important factor in previous pages and is a critical step toward getting your habits to change. Research can keep you motivated.

I believe that you have the power within yourself to make changes. I also believe you all have the power within yourself utilize self-discipline! Research can be done by reading books, listening to TED talks, watching YouTube videos, reading blogs or magazines, consulting with others, hiring a professional, following the topic on social media platforms you are already active on, etc. There is not a wrong way to educate and motivate yourself. The more you interact with the topic, the faster it will grow roots in the forefront of your thinking.

What are some ways to increase your exposure to encouraging content? Take a break now and try to find some online resources from the sources listed above and jot them here so you remember to go back to them:

_____
_____
_____
_____
_____
_____
_____

Toxic positivity

Another habit many of us have that is worth us breaking is toxic positivity. This is one thing you can do to show your kids how to be different and change the generational dynamics that may be occurring in your family is to stop generating toxic positivity. Toxic positivity is a concept that has been increasingly popular over recent years and I think it is crucial that all parents understand what it means. Understanding and reducing your role in promoting toxic positivity will improve your child's understanding of their emotions and their ability to communicate their needs in an effective manner.

Toxic positivity is the concept that being overly positive, optimistic, and/or encouraging can actually be hurtful to the person on the receiving end. When life is difficult for your child and you become Susie Sunshine, approaching them with a cliché such as "*there is always a silver lining*" or "*chin up, buttercup! tomorrow's a new day*" you might notice that they do not seem to appreciate your sentiment. You might even receive negative attitude or aggression from them, why is that? Isn't it a good thing that you are just trying to be positive and encouraging?

You were probably taught in childhood that being endlessly positive is the right thing to do and if other people could only swallow their feelings and put a smile on their faces, it would all be ok! Seems logical, right? Not exactly. When you are trying to be overly positive in the face of another person (including your child's) distress, you are sending them the message that their pain makes you uncomfortable and/or is illogical in the situation. You are doing what you were taught in childhood which is trying to "fix" the situation for your child, you are insisting that they feel better. This is experienced as invalidating to them (which means that you are giving you the message that their interpretation of the situation and/or emotions are wrong). I know this is not what you are intending to do; therefore, I am teaching you about it! When you do what you were taught in childhood and your kiddo does what they think they are supposed to do (i.e.: they think to themselves "*mom is right, I should suck it up...other people have it worse*"), you and they are both invalidating their experience which further compounds the situation. They will grow up unsure if their opinions and interpretations are sensical and can become indecisive and anxious adults. No wonder toxic positivity does not leave anyone feeling better!

One common example that I often see where toxic positivity is on full display, is when kids are going to get their immunizations. The adults try to act cheerful and sing-songy, they tell the kiddo that it will not hurt, or it will barely hurt, and as soon as it is over, they tell the child to *"shake it off"*, *"stop crying"*, *"it is over now"*, etc. If you look at the scenario objectively you might be able to see that their panic and pain are completely valid! They are taken to an appointment that they did not make, as they are being driven there and then examined, they are recalling how painful past shots were and so they do the logical thing, they ask *"do I have to get a shot today?"* You know the answer is (or is likely going to be) *"yes"* but you ignore and/or dance around the topic with *"I'm not sure"* or *"we'll have to wait and see"* or *"yes but only one and they told me it won't hurt today"*. Lies! At the end of the appointment the doctor leaves and says the nurse will be right in with one little shot. The child's anxiety spikes. If the child is young, they tell you how to hold the child down (often including a second person to help hold them down) and the nurse comes in (often with a flat facial expression and is rushed). Everyone holds the child down (who is now probably screaming or freezing in panic) and the shot(s) is jabbed into their leg/arm. No one stopped to teach the child that if they relax their muscles, it will hurt less, no one stopped to teach them breathing or visualization techniques, no one tried distracting them. The band-aids are slapped on and the child and everyone packs up and leaves, never to discuss the experience again. If they child is crying on the way home, they are often consoled half-heartedly and then the situation is ignored or the parent says, *"it wasn't THAT bad"* or *"it's over now"* or *"no more shots for a year!"*. This entire process teaches the child that you cannot be trusted to answer their questions honestly and that they should not even ask. They also learn to bottle up their anxiety as the process unfolds because they have no control. Toxic positivity taught the child that: speaking up is pointless, adults lie, and I must be a baby because they said it should not have hurt. I don't know about you, but if I went through that situation, I'd have a whole lot of emotions: shame at so many people seeing me in my underwear, anger at being lied to, anxiety about strangers holding me down, anger about how badly it hurt, embarrassed about how much I cried or yelled, hurt that my parent tricked me, annoyed at how positive everyone acted, and fear at the soreness I will have tomorrow. The reality is that validating your child's experience will not take away the physical pain, the anxiety, or the shame; however, it will remove the anger they feel toward you and the shame that they might be overreacting while also learning that they can trust you. They will learn that they can bring their big feelings to you without fear of judgment or dismissiveness. I would venture to guess that you want the latter set of outcomes more than the initial set.

I have no problem, and in fact I do encourage people at times to use self-encouragement and positive self-talk to overcome difficulties. Let me explain why that is not hypocritical: It all comes down to intention, mindfulness, and comfort with pain. You can use these three concepts to understand and avoid emotionally hurting your children with toxic positivity. You can stop the pattern of teaching them to ignore their feelings and pretending they are not in emotional pain. To do this, it is important that you remember that pain is relative. This means that while their situation may not cause your adult self to experience pain, it is very real to them. Pain is pain. The pain they feel is the same pain you feel. They cannot be talked out of their pain over a broken toy any more than you could be talked out of the pain of being rejected by a friend.

I hope you are ready to take steps to reverse this trend. When you find yourself leaning into your Suzy Sunshine persona you will first need to stop and evaluate what the intention of your positive statement is? Is it to shut down their emotions? (As mentioned above, that is usually done when the painful emotions make you uncomfortable. If you do not know what to do to help your child feel better, it makes sense that you would try to fix it by being overly encouraging. Unfortunately, that is like putting sprinkles on a pile of poo, not helpful!) Positivity that tries to shut down emotions is toxic positivity. If, on the other hand, the positivity is an effort to try and jazz your little one up in a situation and increase their confidence it can be helpful. You can help them overcome or battle a situation that they are feeling nervous about (such as getting out on the soccer field). That would be healthy and empowering encouragement! Pay attention to the purpose of your words, this is the power of intention.

Second, you need to assess whether your encouraging words are used mindfully or mindlessly? If the words just fly out of your mouth without stopping to check on the intention or outcome, it is likely going to be an invalidating statement which could be perceived as toxic positivity. An example of that is *"you'll be fine..."*. If you say that often, it is mindless, and they know it. If you stop and think "What would I want to hear in this situation? Do their feelings makes sense given their context?" If your words communicate to them that they make sense, then it is likely going to be a more effective comment. An example of that would be *"I know you're feeling nervous about the shots today. They will probably sting. Would you like me to teach you how I breath and what games I like to play in my head while I get shots?"* If you are not sure what to say, it is perfectly acceptable to say out loud *"that is a serious situation, let me think about it for a minute before I respond"* and then take time to think of a helpful answer. That is the power of mindful awareness.

Third, as a parent, you need to understand and work toward acceptance, of pain as a normal part of life. Pain can be quite helpful and will happen to your kids to grow emotionally resilient. You may need to work hard on accepting that being around and sitting with your kids when they are in pain is ok! It is reasonable and acceptable to sit with them in a painful situation, just be in it and let them be in it. It can even be helpful to them to call out what you see "*this situation is difficult*", "*you are feeling really sad*", or "*that was a painful experience*" without trying to swoop in and be the fixer! This is how they will learn the skills they need to overcome difficulties in life. Seeing their pain and naming it for them puts it into perspective, gives it a name, and lets them know that they are not overreacting. As they age, they will learn to problem solve and cope with difficult emotions. In painful moments, I suggest you offer validation statements that communicate the message: *"I see you and it makes sense to me"*) and then zip it. That is all! Practice your own coping skills or your urges to fix the problem or tell them to mask their emotions. Validation communicates to them that their feelings make sense, that they make sense, and that their experience of the world is accurate. You can always ask them if they would like help problem solving the scenario, as long as you can remain open to them saying no.

Here are some examples of toxic positivity and some helpful validating reframing statements to use instead:

Instead of saying: *"Smile/cheer up!"*
Say: *"It's hard to feel that way. I'm here if you'd like to spend some time together"*.

Instead of saying: *"Look for the silver lining!"*
Say: *"Being disappointed is painful."*

Instead of saying: *"You could have it so much worse."*
Say: *"I'm sorry you're experiencing this pain"*

What are some examples you have heard recently (either said to you or things you have said to others)?

_____
_____
_____
_____
_____
_____

As previously mentioned, there is a time and a place for being positive and encouraging, even when your child is expressing a hard emotion. The purpose of this positivity needs to be encouraging them in a situation they in, in which they are capable of the desired outcome. It is also necessary to pair the positivity with validation. An example might be if they are getting ready to perform for the first time and their anxiety is causing them to want to stay home. You could say, *"I think it make sense to feel nervous before going on stage; you might be worried that you will make a mistake. It is normal to make mistakes and it is normal to feel embarrassed when you do. I love you when you make mistakes and when you don't. We will celebrate your performance tonight no matter how it goes!"* Can you imagine how great it would feel if your boss gave you that message?!

Let's recall the name of this chapter: who do you want your kids to become? Teaching your child that they are loved for their efforts, not their outcomes will put them on a lifelong path of healthier self-esteem, willingness to try difficult things and positive connection with you. That sounds like a fantastic outcome!

Their Habits

Now that you understand and are working toward modeling healthier patterns for your kids, you also need to empower them to learn about their own abilities. Kids need chores and responsibility. From the start. Pro-tip: teaching them to do chores will take a bit of work in the beginning (as all new things do); but it will pay off in dividends! Your kids are so much more capable than you give them credit for! When a first grader is learning basic addition or reading skills, an impatient teacher will struggle and want to give them the answers quickly. Seasoned teachers and parents know that the process of teaching them to read or add is time consuming and frustrating at times; however, the long-term goal is worth the short-term difficulties.

I am known for being type-A. I like things to be done a certain way and I am more of a "I'll just do it myself" person than I would like to admit. This pattern can be less than helpful for my children though, and that came into full view for me when one of my daughters was nearing three years old. As I would fold laundry each week, she kept trying to help. Each week I shooed her into the other room to play so I could get it done "correctly" (and quickly). Due to her persistence, it struck me that perhaps she was more capable than I gave her credit for. I decided to take a deep breath and allow her to help me. First, she started by matching the socks and folding the wash cloths. She did GREAT at these tasks after very little practice! I decided at that time to start teaching her some of the basics: to fold a t-shirt (I abandoned my complicated way and told her to fold it in half) and shorts. She also did GREAT at that! During her third year of life, she learned to fold all garments and learned to put them away in the appropriate drawers. It was not perfect, but it dawned on me that neither were her drawers after she searched through them for an item she wanted! Being a behavioral therapist, I knew I needed to reinforce this behavior to encourage it to continue. Each week after she folded her clothes and put them away, I gave her one dollar bill and took her straight to the dollar store nearby (the immediacy of this is critical for human learning). She was on cloud nine choosing her very own item with her very own dollar! Ironically, a washcloth was one of her first purchases.

Empowering your children to help around the house normalizes that a family is a team, shows them how capable they are and removes the pressure that you are putting on yourself to do "all the things".

If you fall into the camp of "I just want them to be kids" and "they deserve to have more fun in their childhood", I want to remind you of some research that was done in the 1970s that has held true through today.

In the 1970s as pop-psychology was born, psychologist/researcher Martin Seligman was conducting new research on learning and ultimately discovered "learned helplessness" and its link to depression. Learned helplessness is a concept that happens when a person discovers (real or imaginary) limitations on their ability to make a change in their world. Have you ever had the thought "Why should I even try? Each time I do, I fail." or "What's the point? I never get it right." Those are examples of learned helplessness. I see this happening a lot with youth when they are not traditional learners…they do their best and it's never good enough! Learned helplessness helped Seligman see that that clinical depression may result from (real or perceived) lack of control over the outcome of a situation. We learn to "give up" and stop trying to influence our environment.

Unfortunately, at the same time as this research, parents were told that kids needed loads of self-esteem. This combination led to the everyone's a winner mentality and was the birth of the participation trophy. The unfortunate consequence has been that kids learned that nothing they did really mattered (i.e.: "It doesn't matter if I try or don't …I'll still get a trophy" or "That person didn't try at all and got the same reward as I did …so why should I try?"). Instead of self-esteem increasing, we saw learned helplessness increase (which can result in higher levels of clinical depression.) The task now, is to teach kids how to struggle and persist through difficult tasks, this will allow them to show themselves that they can do hard things and hard work does pay off and results in higher self-esteem.

Chapter nine will more explicitly address how to start, end, and maintain new behaviors and habits. In the next few chapters, we will address some of the other barriers that impede progress for parents.

Questions to journal on:
1. Who do you visualize your child becoming?
2. What are the things you do that you do not want your child to copy? What things are you doing that you do want them to copy?
3. What sources could you use for inspiration, motivation, and research?
4. What are your thoughts on the topic of toxic positivity? Was it modeled to you in life? How do you feel when people are overly positive to you?
5. Where do you stand on the idea of promoting independence in your children by having them do chores?

3 WHY IS AVOIDANCE SO TEMPTING?

"Avoidance has never been a great tactic in solving any problem. For most situations in life, not addressing what's going on only makes matters worse" – Luvvie Ajayiv

"I don't wanna…"
"Why do I have to…"
"I'd rather…"
"I deserve a break…"
"I'll get to it tomorrow…"

Avoidance can take the shape of many behaviors that you engage in; I find the internal dialogue sounds similar regardless of your tactic. If the above thought examples sound familiar, then I would suggest you take note. Regardless of your go-to avoidance tool (Netflix, video games, alcohol, social media, gossiping, sleep), they all seek to serve one purpose: avoid the discomfort! Avoidance is not always intentional; it can be done inside or outside of your awareness; both are challenging.

Current culture has taken a dramatic turn in the last few decades from having a strong work ethic, to that of an instant-gratification society. The mindset of working for the same company for 30 years and retiring with a pension has evaporated and, in its place, we see the fast-paced entrepreneurial world of startups and self-employment. I do not blame any single industry, cause, or event for this change; rather, I believe it has been a slow erosion over time. I believe it is the result of the chronic gratification culture we live with. As parents, we must recognize the issue and forge onward with a plan to change the course away from frantic efforts to escape boredom, toward life satisfaction and healthy coping. Your kids need life strategies and skills to handle their emotions and urges. As the adult in the situation, I suggest you read my first book <u>Adulting Well: Utilizing the Theories and Strategies of Dialectical Behavioral Therapy</u> first to learn these necessary skills for yourself, so that you can pass the knowledge on to them as a part of your legacy. It is your job as the parent to teach your children how to delay their short-term urges so that they can achieve their long-term goals. The book <u>Adulting Well: Utilizing the Theories and Strategies of Dialectical Behavioral Therapy</u> will teach you what you need to know, in relatable and realistic terms.

Avoidance tends to be the result of an inability for a person to cope with emotional pain and suffering. In order to teach your children the necessary skills for coping with pain, you will first need to learn to experience your own life's pain, cope well, and persist through it. You will first need to learn the benefits of coping with discomfort and the risks of avoidance. Only then can you show your children the path toward emotional freedom, so they do not become dependent on avoidance. You must learn to struggle without giving up or numbing out (I call this successful struggling). When you can turn your negative emotional cycles around, you can teach your children to do the same and all members of your family can have a self-fulfilling prophecy of competence and confidence…instead of being depressed and/or anxious.

You could be avoiding obvious stressors:

- Housework
- Homework
- Sleep
- Your kids
- Your significant other
- Difficult Conversations
- Paying bills or reviewing your budget

Or you could be avoiding less obvious tasks (including healthy coping!):

- Going for a walk
- Exercising
- Painting or crafting
- Reading
- Talking to a friend

A common example of avoidance: screens. If you think of what you are doing when you are watching TV or scrolling on your phone/tablet, the answer is typically some sort of avoidance.

If you compare how you feel after engaging in avoidance vs engaging in effective behavior, I will venture to bet that it is clear which makes you feel better. If you choose an avoidance activity, you are going to feel more depressed, sluggish, unmotivated, lonely, sad, etc. As a result of choosing an effective activity, I'd bet you feel accomplished, productive, proud, happy, relieved, connected (values-based living). On any given day, during any given moment, which would you choose …to feel unmotivated and depressed or to feel productive and happy? Framing it in this way makes it seem silly to choose avoidance. I do believe that choosing to be effective is a simple choice but that does not mean it is an easy one. In fact, it is often painfully difficult! We must confront the fact that when we binge watch shows by the season, we are choosing to feel more sluggish and dejected! Confronting the avoidance will be a struggle and might cause you to feel more fatigued initially.

The benefits of successful struggling are experienced similarly to the benefits of eating your vegetables. You might not like it right away; however, with consistency and time you will notice the benefits. The thought that there are benefits to struggling might sound bizarre; it is counter cultural! Learning to struggle without giving in to your urges to escape will help you:

o Improve self-discipline.
o Discover self-respect.
o Free you from problem behaviors that have plagued you.
o Allow you to feel your emotions, even strong ones, with the self-confidence that you can cope.
o Grow parts of your identity that you previously felt incapable of.
o Improve your relationships.

- o   Gain respect of your family members.

What are your thoughts on "successful struggling", what do you want to gain from learning to manage your struggles more successfully?

_____
_____
_____
_____
_____
_____

You may find that you get yourself into trouble when you avoid dealing with an issue, it may be easier in the short term but then the problems get bigger. Coping by using avoidance is a maladaptive coping skill that many people have learned over the years. Avoidance means that you pretend that a real issue isn't such a big deal. As a parent, I see this being very applicable with a child's behavioral problems. If not caught and addressed early on, they can spiral out of control. Your first goal is to realize when you are avoiding …and then take actions to avoid avoiding!

One of the great truths in life is that you will pay for your choices. You can choose to pay on the front end and reap the rewards later, or you can choose to take the easy route initially and pay a cost on the back end. One example of this is when it comes to health: you can pay up front by eating in a healthful way and exercising regularly which allows you to reap the benefits of better health over your lifespan and more energy as you age or you can ignore all of the warnings and live a fun life of eating fast food, drinking sugary drinks, and avoiding the gym through your teens and twenties, only to discover the ramifications (and their cost) on your health in later decades. Another, perhaps more important example, is as it relates to parenting. You can pay up front with diligent effort with boundaries and teaching healthy habits to your child from birth through middle school and reap the benefits of a healthier, more stable teen or you can give in and let your little one have what they want when they are young, only to realize that it's much harder to reign it in when they are older! A final, easy example would be with car maintenance. Do you want to pay up front for oil changes and routine maintenance or do you want to enjoy the saved money for the first few years only to have your car break down and leave you needing a new one? Avoidance keeps us comfortable in the short-term, yet leaves us very uncomfortable later on!

As we have already explored in the last chapter, creating new habits is not always easy. There will be a requirement for you to be consistent and continually practice the skill. There will be an expectation that you can accept and not beat yourself up for the inevitable failures that will happen along the way. You may need to revisit this chapter for motivation. <u>It takes time for your body to develop muscle memory or grow muscular strength; in the same way, it takes time for new habits to be comfortable.</u>

Coping With Your Urges to Avoid

When you are teetering on the edge of giving-in and avoiding your thoughts and emotions you have several options for coping as outlined below. You will have urges to give up and avoid along the way and planning to cope effectively and succeed will decrease the likelihood that you give into avoidance behaviors.

Internal Mantra

An internal mantra can go a long way! Internal mantras are ways that you can encourage yourself and have a pre-planned statement ready to use when your emotions try to convince you to give into their urges. I think of an internal mantra as a sort of "press-release" for the internal toddler that we all have! You know that your internal toddler will push back against change, especially when you are hungry, angry, lonely, and tired. Here are some examples of prepared press-release statements that you could borrow or adapt for yourself:

- o This, too, shall pass.
- o Do it for your future.
- o Do something your future self will be proud of.
- o Watch me!
- o I am sick and tired of being sick and tired.
- o I am worth this.
- o Wise mind can wait.
- o Slow and steady wins the race.

- I have a choice.
- It will get better.
- I got this.
- Nothing lasts forever.
- I can and I will.

What are your encouraging internal mantras?
_____
_____
_____
_____
_____
_____

Self-Encouragement

 A close cousin to use alongside of or instead of a personal mantra is self-encouragement. I am astounded at how hard people are on themselves compared to how gentle and forgiving they can be of others. The basic premise of self-encouragement is that your internal dialogue needs to be in alignment with how you would speak to a friend, neighbor, elderly person, or child. Take a moment to reflect on those categories. Which one holds a tender place in your heart? (Hint: that's the one to use!) When a friend comes to you with a struggle, I would venture to believe that you are supportive, encouraging, validating, and nurturing. When interacting with an elderly person, I'd guess you are more compassionate and understanding than you are with yourself. When talking with a child, I'd bet you are more patient and nurturing. Take any of those qualities and start using them on yourself!

 The way you speak to yourself will either improve your emotional wellbeing or cause you to spiral downward. I doubt you would ever tell a friend or your kids the same types of negative statements that you say to yourself. If your child came crying to you about a real-life problem, I doubt you would say, "*suck it up*", "*get over it*", "*what's wrong with you*", etc.…So why on earth would you say those things to yourself? Your kids are listening to you, and they hear the things you say about yourself as a parent. They hear you judging yourself when you are on the phone with a friend and that can become their own internal dialogue. Furthermore, would you keep a friend around who talked to you in that way? I do not think so. I think you would avoid them like the plague.

Self-encouragement suggests that you act and surround yourself with cues that might remind you to be a bit kinder to yourself. You can find ideas for how to do this by using these suggestions:

- Print out cutesy encouraging phrases.
- Follow inspirational people on social media.
- Splurge on that wall art that moves you.
- Set the backdrop of your phone and/or laptop to be motivational.
- Use a dry erase marker on your mirrors.
- Use bathtub crayons in your shower.
- Buy a positive thought-a-day calendar.
- Buy the jewelry with the catchy calming or motivating phrase on it.

What is a self-encouraging statement and how can you be sure to see it regularly?

_____
_____
_____
_____
_____
_____

Personal Space

When you are feeling overstimulated, overwhelmed, or otherwise overly emotional, you need space from the triggers and the risky choices that you are wanting to make. I know it may seem too hard to find space; however, it is a great skill to model for your kids!

If you are feeling overwhelmed and are worried that you cannot continue to be effective, you need to get some space from everyone, including your children. You could say to them "*I need to calm down because I am feeling overwhelmed. I am going to take a shower and then we can talk about this. I would like for you to have quite play time in your room for 10 minutes and then I will be in to talk".* With almost every urge you are struggling with, this space will provide you with physical and mental space to re-calibrate and come back to your internal wisdom.

Having space from your risky choices and temptations will require you to assess your behavioral patterns mindfully and honestly. You need to know what you are likely to reach for when you avoid. If you are having urges to "unwind" with alcohol, then you need to get space from alcohol. Try not to keep it in your home and do not let your emotions convince you that you "need" to run to the store for something else

Where is your safe space?
_____
_____
_____
_____
_____
_____

Schedules

Keeping a schedule is a required element of avoiding avoidance. When I think back over the last few years about when I felt the most productive and confident, I readily identify the winter between 2012/2013. I can also easily identify why…I had a great schedule! I was honoring myself by going to the gym, visiting family, spending time with friends, and working with regularity and consistency. Having a schedule prevented me from overworking, isolating, and/or avoiding. I was able to meet my own needs and take care of myself by relying on a schedule that I made while in my wisest state of mind. Ensuring that you make time for yourself will allow you to cope with more dissatisfaction of the day with more success as you are keeping yourself emotionally level throughout the week.

I recommend that you stick to your schedule for several weeks before making any changes. At first, only make changes to things that were problematic during your trial run. This might be removing things that you scheduled after work if you find yourself having to stay late at work certain days. It may be permitting yourself to sleep in on a

Thursday or Friday if your week is taxing. Try to limit the number of changes you make at a time so that you know what is helping the most. Limiting the variables will help you to identify which factors matter more than others.

Do you have a schedule? What gets in the way of sticking to it?
_____
_____
_____
_____
_____
_____

As much as it pains me to admit it, my effective schedule includes:
- Waking up before my house wakes up (I shoot for 5:45am) 4 days per week
- Going to the gym on those days from 6-7am
- Getting everyone and everything ready for the day between 7-9am
- Working from 9-5 (give or take)
- Dinner 5-6
- Family time 6-7:30
- Time with my spouse 8-9:30pm

A few things we do to ensure this can happen are that we meal prep on Sundays so that most nights, dinner is premade. My husband and I have both found that time alone is important. Our alone time happens at the gym, out with our own friends, and/or spending time alone on the weekends hiking, shopping, reading, and on solo long weekend trips. These behaviors do require effort initially, but they allow us to have a comfortable week which is well worth it!

As with all therapy and strategies, these ideas only work if you work and put in the time and effort needed. You will need to put in mental and physical effort throughout this journey. Change does not happen overnight. If there was a self-help book that had all the answers or a pill that fixed everything, I would tell you and gladly retire! Parenting and coping with urges to avoid will require sustained effort and diligence before it gets easier.

Questions to journal on:

1. What are my "red flag" thoughts/statements/behaviors that I engage in when I avoid?
2. Has my internal dialogue been cheering me on, or putting me down?
3. Do I feel comfortable asking for space when I am overwhelmed? Why is that?

4 DEALING WITH EMOTIONS

"Negative emotions like loneliness, envy, and guilt have an important role to play in a happy life; they're big, flashing signs that something needs to change" – Gretchen Rubin

Let's face it. Parenting is HARD with a capital H. Parenting takes a level of sustained energy from the parent that seems (and often is) unrealistic. The toll that this can take on the body and psyche are no joke. If a parent has already had a rough day or is already vulnerable due to things like financial stress, social discord, chronic pain, or other medical issues, etc. they are more likely to be worn down by their kid's (age-appropriate) needs and behaviors. A worn-down parent is likely to be irritable and engage in power struggles; a typical child is likely to react to this negativity and a negative spiral ensues. I am sure you can imagine where that spiral is likely to end.

An encouraging bit of news is that a study in 2005 found that people who can effectively regulate their emotions tend towards better physical health (Carre et al, 2005), and another found that people with effective emotion regulation abilities report higher levels of relationship qualities (Levenson et al, 1994). I have certainly experienced both findings to be true in my life and the lives of my clients. I hope that these simple facts can provide added motivation for you to do the hard work outlined in this book. Learning to regulate our emotions without quick-fixes or avoidance will open the door and allow us to walk towards the goals we have set for our future selves more efficiently.

How do you feel about the idea that your child feeds from your energy and vice versa?

_____
_____
_____
_____
_____
_____
_____
_____
_____
_____
_____
_____
_____
_____
_____
_____
_____
_____
_____
_____
_____
_____
_____
_____
_____

My experience as a therapist has shown me that emotional IQ in our world is lacking. Our society tends to struggle with identifying what they are feeling aside from the simplest versions of happy, mad, sad, and scared. Emotional IQ allows you to go beyond happy and elaborate as to whether you are feeling loving, hopeful, confident, optimistic, playful, thankful, etc. We can learn to be more specific about our anger and state that we are bitter, skeptical, resentful, jealous, or frustrated. It would be helpful to those around you to learn about the complexities of emotions because instead of saying you are scared, you could clarify if you are feeling threatened, helpless, nervous, or anxious. And in the same trend, you can elaborate on sadness and describe whether your feeling despair, emptiness, abandonment, or grief. Learning the depths of emotions and how to be clearer about what you are feeling will allow others to know how to approach you and communicate with you with more success. It is also a fantastic life skill to model for your kids! Emotional IQ was not a priority in the world prior to the industrial revolution because the fixation was on survival and people were far too exhausted by their laborious jobs. Post-industrial revolution brought on other fears as a result of the Great Depression, World War I and II, threats of a cold war, etc. Psychology and related research finally had a chance to blossom in the 1900s and as such, the results of said research did not start to take-hold until the late 1900s. Now it is our responsibility to carry forward the need for increased emotional IQ and healthier connections with our children through attachment, bonding, modeling, and teaching!

My favorite tool for increasing emotional literacy is to use a "feelings wheel" to illustrate the layers of emotion. The exact origin of the feelings wheel is up for debate; it is credited to have been the brain child of Joseph Zinker in the late 1970s, to Robert Plutchik in 1980, and to psychotherapist Gloria Willcox in the 1980s. Geoffrey Roberts has updated and published a comprehensive feelings wheel which is shown here (reprinted with permission from Geoffrey Roberts):

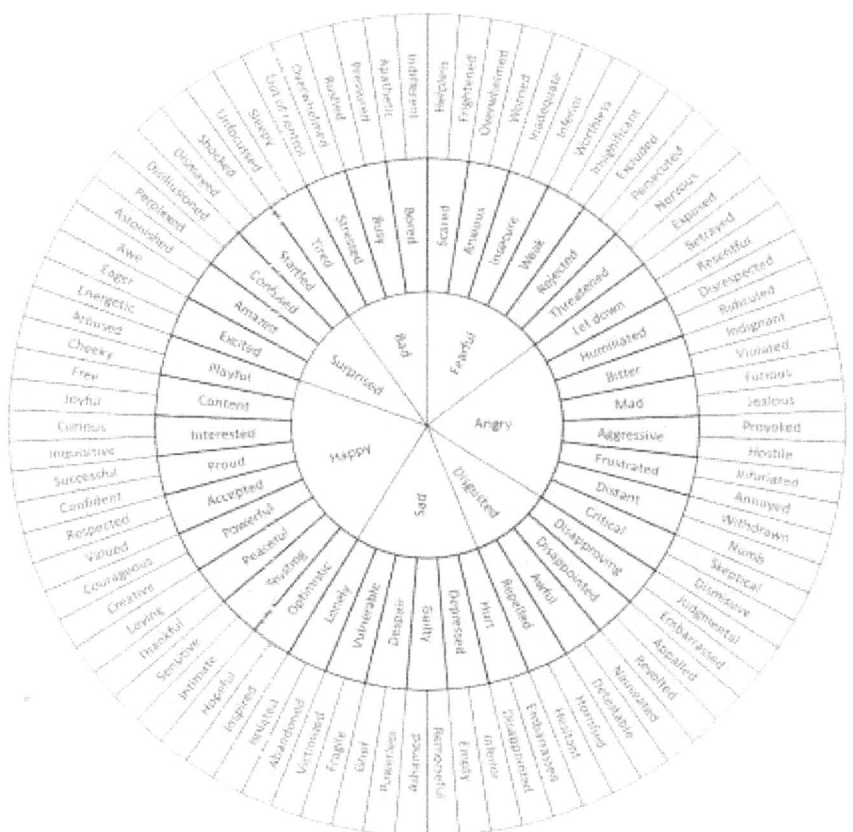

Color versions of the feelings wheel can also be helpful tools, as each core emotions and their secondary and tertiary emotions are all shaded in different colors, so that the wheel resembles a pie with different colored slices. I encourage you to color this one in, take time to identify what colors you associate with the core emotions and color the pie slice outward from the inner circle. For example, I associate yellow with happy, red with anger, blue with sad, etc. It can also be a great practice for your family to discuss. You may find that your child or spouse would use different colors to represent emotions than you chose. Allow conversation to flow with curiosity!

I encourage you to reference the feelings wheel often and learn how to accurately communicate your experiences; thus, showing your children how to do the same! You could also print one from the internet or purchase a feelings wheel poster to have in your home for reference. As you become more familiar with this wheel, you will be able to elaborate on your emotional experience. Instead of saying you're "angry" about a scenario, try tuning in a bit more accurately and take ownership of your emotion of bitterness, jealousy, or perhaps frustration. Instead of using "I'm happy" as a blanket statement for all positive experiences, you can elaborate and let people know that you are feeling optimistic, loving, or proud. This will help other people relate to you easier and respond to you in ways that allow for deeper connection. Imagine the decrease of overthinking you could do if other people communicated so clearly with you!

Which sections of the emotion wheel do you feel more comfortable with? Which sections seemed foreign to you?

_____
_____
_____
_____
_____
_____
_____
_____
_____
_____
_____
_____
_____
_____
_____

Do you think things would be different if you and your family members could communicate more clearly about how you are feeling? If so, how?

_____
_____
_____
_____

Awareness of Red Flags

As you learn to identify the core emotion that you are struggling with, you will also learn to identify the emotional experience sooner. You can learn to see the signs of loneliness prior to falling completely into a pit of despair. You can learn to spot the signs of irritability prior to losing your temper and screaming at your children. There is power in opening your eyes to the ways your body, thoughts, and urges are giving you clues throughout the day! Muscle tension urges for sugary snacks, low energy, stomach upset, and/or an inability to sit still are all examples of cues you can look for that you are on your way to a stronger emotional upset.

What are the signs of emotional struggles you have? Do you often ignore them or do you feel tuned into your mind-body connection?

When you are having a tough day with your kids, it will be easy to fall into distraction or a self-deprecating internal dialogue. Distracting yourself by streaming television shows, drinking a glass of wine, or escaping into social media will only lead to a delayed explosion (such as a fight with your kids the next morning at breakfast). Beating yourself up and judging your parenting will keep you stuck in a shame-cycle and can also result in a delayed explosion (such as a fight with your significant other). This chapter is all about learning to interact with your emotions in healthier ways, to stop that emotional snowball from rolling downhill!

You might be being overwhelmed after a tough day of parenting if you experience any of these symptoms:

- Losing temper
- You get "touched out" (meaning you do not want any more physical touch)
- You need alone time
- You feel as if you are going to "explode" from pressure
- You feel like you need to "hide" from your kids
- Picking fights with other people
- Ruminating on how irritated you are (having the same thoughts stuck in your head).

What are the symptoms you experience when you are overwhelmed?

_____
_____
_____
_____
_____

Do you find yourself swinging from one extreme to another? "I'm getting so much done" to "I've done nothing today"? Do you find yourself saying statements such as "I can't handle this"! or "this is too hard"? In these example statements, it might be easier for you to see the intensity and absolute nature of the statements. Thinking in all-or-nothing absolutes will not help you and should be a big red flag. The reality is that very few things are "always" or "never"!

I tend to hear two extremes from people when they are in low-mood places. People either get overwhelmed and channel that into anxious mania and get so much done or they fall into fatalistic thinking and give up, laying round binge-watching reruns all day.

Do you try to "keep up with the Jones's, Pinterest Moms, Type-A friends in your social media feed? Do you stress out about accomplishing everything that's been on your to-do list? Do you try to take advantage of and make time for all the free classes, podcasts, blogs, and books that people discuss? Be careful because if this is you, you will hit a wall (and it's a brick wall).

Conversely, when you are overwhelmed do you find it to be an excuse to stay in your pajamas, eat all the snacks, and watch endless hours of streamed TV? Do you skip showers and avoid anything that resembles a routine? Be careful because if this is you, you will fall into the pit (and it's a muddy, mucky pit).

Which patterns described above are you more likely to fall into?

_____
_____
_____
_____
_____
_____
_____
_____
_____
_____
_____
_____
_____
_____
_____
_____

It's crucial that you are kind to yourself and develop the ability to self-validate and self-encourage the difficulties you experience. Some examples of that include saying to yourself:

- "I am tired from _____ and that makes sense, today I'll take it easy"
- "I have enjoyed a few days of relaxation and now I am

ready to tackle one thing off of my list"
- "I am worthy of a break"
- "My ideas are worth working toward"

Reframing your goals as a parent will require you to think in different ways. Trying to be perfect does not work. One day, if I am famous for saying anything, it will be for saying *"there is no right answer; there is a more effective answer for you to reach your goals"*. Reframing your goals away from absolutes and more into a grey zone can help you get, and stay, unstuck.

One example of an area to work on finding balance is how you spend your time. If you have been working hard, it is perfectly acceptable to take some time off and relax. If you have just come to the surface after binge-watching 3 seasons of something, it might be time to organize your sock drawer and alphabetize your DVD collection! I think our children need to see how to live the balance and how to course-correct when they've fallen to one extreme or the other! I like to use a metaphor of a teeter totter, if you constantly flip from one side to the other you will exhaust yourself! Part of living in the middle is learning to stand on top of the teeter totter plank and dance in the middle – acknowledging that it will dip to each side, it will crash on each side, and yet our goal is to get right back to the center.

Rebounding from Overstimulation

If that felt a bit too much like looking in the mirror, there is good news: there is a lot of hope! There are many options for ways to cope, rebound, and build resilience which will help you gain the confidence necessary to tackle parenting effectively again. Here are some helpful strategies to implement which will allow you to rebound after a difficult day:

1. Learn to speak up! You can teach your children about your boundaries, which in turn teaches them to be aware of theirs! You can teach them what sorts of things you would prefer them to do in other rooms vs in your presence. You can teach them to turn the volume down or turn off noise producing devices when they are finished so there are not several going at once. You can inform your family and friends not to

purchase certain items (toys or food) for your kids as well if they tend to cause fights or stress. You can speak to your family members/spouse about your needs and ask them to understand if you need a break (including a break from them). Figuring out your triggers and making them known in your home is something you have a right to do and is something your family members have a right to know about.

2. Be willing to prioritize your down/alone time. Ways to achieve this are to be sure that someone relieves you and you go for a walk to clear your mind, you can lock the doors during a shower, utilize the kids club at a fitness center, and enforce quiet time for all members of your home to be in their rooms once or twice per day (be consistent about this as it will take time for everyone to adjust).
3. Change the internal dialogue. Instead of trying to tell yourself to "suck it up" or that you must be "crazy", be kinder with your self-talk and remember that you are not the only person who experiences being overwhelmed! Go back to chapter three and review the self-encouraging press release statements and write one on your bathroom mirror, on a post-it note that you place in your car or make it the backdrop of your cell phone! Honor your needs and remember that judging and blaming yourself will only keep you stuck in a shame spiral, which will promote more problematic behavior.
4. If household noises contribute to the overwhelming feelings you experience, you can wear noise dampening earbuds to block out some of the less intense noises. It is especially helpful to use them in the later hours of the day as your children's whining increases and your nerves are more frayed.
5. Get outside (yes, even with the kids) and mindfully turn your attention toward any nature you can see (a rock, a blade of grass, a cloud in the sky, a bird, etc.), this gives your brain a break from the chaos and allows you to focus on something else. There is more content on mindfulness in chapter eight which will be helpful to use when engaging with nature!
6. Engage your five senses in soothing activities such as lotioning, using an essential oil diffuser, drinking hot tea, looking at beautiful art, etc. You can even train yourself to use a certain tool as a catalyst for calm, so that they experiences associated

with it (such as the peppermint smell of a stick of gum, the mug's warmth of hot tea, certain colors you see often when observing nature) can become classically conditioned in your brain as relaxing!

When it comes to being overwhelmed, it is important to dig a bit deeper into the idea of coping with our sensory system. I want you to imagine that your physical sensations and emotional experiences are hard wired together in your brain. Think about it as the DNA double helix, this idea can have huge mental health implications. Consider the last time you were upset, emotional, or impulsive. I would venture to guess that you were not easily reasoned with at that time. It is common for family and friends to try and logically tell you how to "calm down" in those moments, but we all know that it is not helpful. Instead of being talked at, you are likely to be soothed more successfully using the other strand in your double helix – the physical sensation side – to sooth yourself. When your emotions are raw, instead of attacking them directly, you can attack them via physical sensations as a shortcut. Any sensory activity that you find pleasing can be a direct path to emotional relief. Think about how well you do this with your child (especially when they were young). You probably gave them binkies, blankies, and/or stuffed animals. You may have turned on a sound machine or visually soothing mobiles. You probably sang to them, rocked, and patted them. You did all those things because they work! The theory I ask you to apply is the same with your adult self (refer to number six above) and items that you find pleasing: lotions, candles, warm baths, relaxing instrumental music, soft blankets, hot tea, etc.

7. Consult with professionals: occupational therapy, speech therapy, mindfulness-based therapies and cognitive behavioral therapies can all be useful tools for parenting issues. If you find yourself unable to downregulate when you are keyed up, you may find the help of a massage therapist, a mental health therapist or a holistic practitioner such as reiki or acupuncture professional to be helpful tools. When symptoms are interfering greatly with your quality of life, you have a right to investigate treatment options with the help of a professional!

Which of these seven strategies will you try? Which feel too unachievable?

_____
_____
_____
_____
_____
_____
_____
_____
_____
_____
_____
_____
_____
_____
_____

The Power of Words

As mentioned above, we need to change the internal narrative. It is crucial that you learn to be kind to yourself through self-validation, self-compassion, and self-encouraging language and thinking. Your kids are watching, and they will learn the same language and skills. If you talk harshly to yourself *(I.e.: "what the hell is wrong with me?!" Or "I could never _____")* then they are likely to do the same. I will never forget when I was sitting with my daughter, and she was trying to do math homework in second grade. It was difficult and she finally cried out *"I suck"*! I was taken aback and began wondering where she heard this. To my relief, I am confident that she did not pick it up from me as it is not a phrase I say. The reality is that she heard it from someone; she picked up someone else's negative self-talk and internalized it. I worked with her on reframing it into *"this is hard"*, *"I am frustrated"* and encouraged her to take a break for a while as to not fall further into the spiral. You likely have similar internal dialogue, and your child will pick it up from you. Healthier language that you could practice saying to yourself includes self-validating statements and self-encouraging statements.

Your internal dialogue will be influenced by your past experiences in childhood, your present circumstances, and your fears of the future. Your internal dialogue can be healthy or unhealthy; most people experience both. In places where your dialogue frequently turns negative, the content from chapter five will be helpful. In the same way that an athlete or performer must practice repeatedly, you will need to practice breaking the habit of negative self-talk and replacing it with more neutral or positive dialogue.

Is your internal dialogue healthy or unhealthy? Do you have any ideas about where your internal dialogue came from?

_____
_____
_____
_____
_____
_____
_____
_____
_____
_____
_____
_____
_____
_____
_____
_____
_____
_____

The Power of Action:

If you have ever experienced a bout of depression, I am sure you have heard (once or twice) that you should exercise to improve your mood. That advice is not wrong; and yet, it is not easy. I am here to let you know that there is another powerful antidote for depression which may feel more achievable, and it takes the form of the DBT (Dialectical Behavioral Therapy) skill of *BUILDing MASTERY*.

Build Mastery is a very small skill in the DBT manual (which makes me sad) but it packs a powerful punch. To build mastery is to spend time developing a skill/talent/hobby/activity and becoming mindfully aware of your progress over time.

In reading about this skill, I want you to use this table as your guide:

Too Easy	No effect, could backfire and make you feel infantilized
Challenging	Builds self-worth/self-esteem
Too Hard	Likely leads to you feeling incompetent

For success and to achieve the antidepressant effect, the task you choose to engage in will need to fall in the middle row: challenging. An example might be to run a 5k marathon for a generally healthy and uninjured adult. If you decide, with no prior training, to run a full marathon, you are likely to injure yourself, fail, and probably feel worse about yourself. That is not because you are a failure, it is because you choose something that was a bit too much of a leap, it was a bit too hard. If you choose to walk 10 paces forward, you are unlikely to feel any sense of accomplishment because that is too easy! You will not continue to work toward your goal of running and therefore will feel like the exercise was pointless if you choose something that is too hard or too easy. The sweet spot involves breaking your goal of running a 5k into reasonable and tangible steps (such as researching and purchasing running shoes, finding local trails/parks, finding a running plan, or joining a running club, sharing your plan with others, beginning to work up to short jogs and slowly lengthening the distance.

If you hate running and now you are angry that I suggested it, have no fear because you can build mastery in almost any area!

- o Gardening.
- o Cleaning.
- o Sewing.
- o Painting.
- o Learning a language.
- o Computer coding.
- o Playing strategy games.
- o Cooking or baking.

- Any sport.
- Reading (longer books, more complex books).
- Home repairs and DIY projects.
- Budgeting.
- Crafting.
- Weaning yourself from soda to water.
- Changing how you parent your children.
- Implementing the ideas explained earlier in this chapter to cope with your overwhelm.

What areas could you work to build mastery in?

_____
_____
_____
_____
_____
_____

Questions to journal on:

1. What are my tell-tale symptoms or signs that I am reaching my breaking point?
2. What are some readily available tools I could use to cope in my environment?
3. What is one way I could speak up or self-advocate within my home to reduce my stress?
4. What are some areas that you find yourself being "all-or-nothing" in your thinking?
5. Is your internal dialogue encouraging you to try again or is it belittling you and keeping you stuck in feelings of failure? List a few encouraging statements you could practice saying to yourself.
6. What is one area you would be willing to try to build mastery? Identify a goal that is too easy, challenging, and too hard.

5 SELF-WORTH, SELF-LOVE, AND SELF-CONFIDENCE

"Love Yourself First and everything else falls into line. You really have to love yourself to get anything done in this world" – Lucille Ball

When you are having a difficult time emotionally it is so easy to fall into the pit of despair, the "it's not fair" lifestyle, and the "woe is me" attitude. We have established that parenting is hard, and you will have days that tip you into an unpleasant mental state. I do not need to tell you that it is pointless to go there; stagnation does not produce growth. Staying stuck does not help anyone. To improve your self-esteem, you need to wake up to your life and notice that that we have choices. Every single moment of our life presents us with choices, parenting is no different.

I absolutely love when someone tells me that I cannot do something. I have a rebellious streak and I am quick to adopt the "watch me" mentality when someone doubts me. I want to empower you too, to adopt a strong mind frame because you are not a weak or incapable parent.

You are:

- A role model to your child(ren).
- A strong independent parent.
- A proud survivor of your own life circumstances.
- A motivator.
- A teacher.

- A brilliant thinker
- A coach.
- An individual.
- A friend.

The hurricanes that life has thrown at you are an amazing gift because they made you who you are! You became all these things out of the struggles you endured. They made you stronger and more resilient. Embrace the struggles in life and have faith that you will come through them, and you will be able to help others once you are on the other side.

I want you to adopt the mentality of rising-up. Being a parent who can see the growth possibilities in life and take hold of them. I see my role here as being a hand that reaches down into the dust of the depression pit, into the chaos of an anxious mind and reaches through the brick walls of anger in an effort of helping each parent reading to have better mental health.

The primary goal of this chapter is to help you learn the difference between self-love, self-worth, and self-confidence and how to improve all three.

Are you willing to shift your mentality and rise to a place of self-confidence? What has stopped you over the years?

_____
_____
_____
_____
_____
_____
_____
_____
_____
_____
_____
_____
_____
_____

Self-Worth

Worth is the value of something placed on it by society or yourself. Worth is subjective and is up for discussion which is why some people have a difficult time believing a compliment.

I am sure you can think of an item you own (or owned in the past, even as a child) that you placed more worth on than society would have, it came from within. For me, I have had a treasured rock collection, special tattered quilts, and I currently still have a Fozzie Bear Muppet Baby figurine that is precious to me from my childhood. I place high worth on them, and I am aware that other people may not find them to be worth anything at all.

Improving your self-worth must come from within. You will need to determine that you are worthy of your own time, attention, and resources and until you do that, it is likely that others will ignore your requests and will see you as a push-over. People with low self-worth often make jokes at their own expense and are not likely to speak up for their preferences. If others laugh along at the jokes or do not pick up on minor preferences that are casually mentioned, the person uses their confirmation bias to determine that it is proof of their low worth. I mentioned earlier in the book that I would use your love for your children to manipulate you: this chapter is one place I will do that. If you want your children to have healthy self-worth, you must lead by example.

Self-esteem and self-worth can be thought of as synonymous. Self-esteem cannot be bought; it must be earned. That means that unless you set a goal and struggle to reach it (be that at work, with parenting, in a hobby, financially, etc.), you will not feel good about yourself.

Ideas for Raising your Self-Worth:

o   Treat your body as a sacred place.

This means that you recognize the mind-body connection and treat your physical body accordingly. You understand that chronic stress and anger take a dramatic toll on your physical and emotional well-being. You can reverse that toll by taking the steps that you know lead to healthier life.
- Stop smoking and/or vaping.

- Exercise regularly.
- Drink water as a primary beverage.
- Go for walks.
- Stretch.
- Eat fruits and vegetables every day.
- Limit fast food and junk food.
- Visit the dentist twice per year and the primary care doctor yearly.

To prioritize any of the mentioned suggestions here for healthier living forces you to engage in an action that only someone who thinks their life is worthy would do. You might have to "fake it" initially, but I know that over time you will develop a sense of pride over the healthy choices you are making. In time, that pride will increase your self-worth!

How have you been treating your body? What small changes can you make to support increased self-worth?

_____
_____
_____
_____
_____
_____
_____
_____
_____
_____
_____
_____
_____
_____
_____
_____

o Values-based living.

Values-based living is a concept that I introduced in chapter one.

If you have time, go back, and re-read that section and see if you have taken any strides toward values-based living in the time it has taken you to read the last 4 chapters. If you have not taken any actions that are aligned with your previously identified values, that is ok! That might be a sign to pick a different value to start with, to recommit to your prior plan, or to evaluate what got in your way and problem solve it.

Living according to your values raises your self-worth because it is not always a convenient thing to do, and yet you are taking actions that tell yourself and the world, that you are worth it. You are worth your own time, attention, and resources.

What is a small step you could take to increase values-based living?

_____
_____
_____
_____
_____
_____
_____
_____
_____
_____
_____
_____
_____
_____
_____

- Journal and meditate.

Self-reflection is not something a person does if they think they are worthless. They do not believe their thoughts, time or attention are worthy of evaluation or recording on paper. They believe they are disposable and that others see them as disposable. I hope that you do not believe those things about yourself.

Journaling can help us to see patterns in our thinking and your behaviors. When we find problematic patterns, we can journal to explore solutions and problem solving. In doing so, you give yourself the message that your problems are worth solving, your moods are worth improving, and your relationships are worth saving. There is more information on journaling in chapter seven.

Meditation achieves a similar result without the writing. When you meditate in any fashion (such as clearing the mind, listening to a meditation recording, focusing on a mantra or affirmation, praying, etc.) you will generally find a sense of peace and clarity that seems to magically improve your abilities to cope, and problem solve. You would not take time for such an activity if you did not believe you deserved such an experience. I believe that meditating and journaling on a regular basis will improve your self-worth because they are actions that tell yourself that you are worth your own time and energy!

Are you willing to try new things like journaling and meditation? Consider practicing by answering these prompts below:
My thoughts on journaling are…
Meditation is…

_____
_____
_____
_____
_____
_____
_____
_____
_____
_____
_____
_____
_____
_____
_____
_____
_____
_____

o   Celebrate your wins (somewhat unapologetically).

People who have low self-esteem feel ashamed and embarrassed by their accomplishments. They are likely to think that they do not deserve celebration and/or their success was a fluke. If you fall into this category, you will need to practice acknowledging that you worked hard and that your success was earned, and you will need to accept compliments and/or praise from others with a "thank you" and not a self-deprecating remark. Your success is just as well earned as anyone else's. You made the choices in life that yielded the results you have; when it pans out in your favor, accept the congratulations from others and pat yourself on the back, a simple "thank you" is a great place to start!

What is something you are proud of about yourself?

_____
_____
_____
_____
_____
_____
_____
_____
_____
_____
_____
_____
_____
_____
_____
_____
_____

Self-Love

Self-love is the degree to which you feel deep affection for yourself as a person. It includes interest and pleasure in your own personality as well as having regard for your own happiness and wellness. Self-love is not something frequently discussed at family dinners and throughout childhood; as such, it is a foreign topic to many.

Self-love as a parent can be difficult as most parents find endless reasons to beat themselves up because they had an episode of parenting in ways that they are not proud of. The reality is that we all have slip ups in our behavior, I urge you not to hold yourself to any standard that you would not also hold a friend to. Self-love as a parent would include an internal dialogue that is less abusive and more compassionate toward yourself.

If you re-read the definition from the first paragraph under self-love, you can see a set of topics to think over which might help you evaluate your own self-love:

- Do you like who you are?
- Are you proud of who you are?
- Do you enjoy spending time alone with yourself?
- Do you take time to evaluate your own desires and level of happiness?
- Are you able to prioritize things that are important to you?

_____
_____
_____
_____
_____
_____

Ideas for Improving Self-love:

- Stop comparing yourself to others.

    The reality is that all people have a hang-up with at least one part of their appearance and/or personality. I have worked with people from all walks of life, and I have worked with kids/teens who were raised in all sorts of different homes and family types. No one and no way are perfect. There are many ways to parent, many ways to dress, many careers to choose from, etc. No one loves every choice they make! Instead of using comparison as a weapon against yourself and against connection with others, you need to work on acceptance of your life and appearance as they currently are. Placing more value on other's opinions (or what you think other's opinions are) is toxic and dangerous to your self-worth and ability to love yourself. To stop comparing yourself to others may require you to delete or step away from social media.

What are you working on accepting (instead of torturing yourself with comparison)?
_____
_____
_____
_____
_____
_____

- Practice loving yourself.

    Practice is required if you want to make new habits. To practice loving yourself means that you are taking time to identify things that you do love about yourself, decisions you have made that you are proud of and parts of your life that you do find to be satisfying. That is a choice you can make. There is a metaphor that I use in therapy a lot: we can all look out the same window and see something different. You have a choice between looking at the litter, telephone wires, and asphalt or you can choose to see the sky, trees, and birds. You can use this same idea when looking at yourself. You can choose to see the parts you like instead of fixating on the parts you don't. Choose kindness toward yourself.

o   Be willing to prioritize your needs.

Prioritizing your own needs means that you are willing to evaluate your schedule, finances, needs, etc. and are willing to tell friends, family, and/or your job that you cannot do something they are asking you to do, if after a cost-benefit analysis, you determine that it would not be wise to you. To say "no" to plans might feel wrong initially and will take time to get used to. You are prioritizing yourself right now by reading this book, give yourself some credit for that!

Going a bit further, prioritizing your needs might mean that you need to remove toxic people from your life or distance yourself from people who are not helping you grow in a healthy direction. Relationships change over time, and it is not guaranteed to be for the best. Be open to evaluating your connections periodically and asking yourself if they are helping you be an emotionally healthy and mature parent or if they are holding you back. It is ok to take a previously close friend and allow them to drift out to being an acquaintance or vice versa.

What is one simple way you can prioritize your needs this week?
_____
_____
_____
_____
_____
_____

- Feel your feelings and think your thoughts without judgment or overly identifying with them.

Thoughts and emotions are not inherently bad or dangerous. They are impulses in your brain, some can be measured on brain scans, and yet they cannot harm you. They can lead you to have urges to engage in actions that harm you or your relationships. Anger, for example, is not dangerous. It signals you to the fact that something is not going your way or a goal you have is being blocked. If anger at your child leads to any type of mistreatment, it is a problem. For example, while raising your voice at your child is not ideal, if done occasionally, it is not mistreatment. If you find yourself using hurtful language, shaming, or insulting your child, that would be mistreatment and I would suggest that you seek professional intervention in order to make change as quickly as possible.

Learning to see your thoughts as thoughts, your urges as urges, and your emotions as emotions can help you get clarity and not act on each one that you have! This concept will take practice and becomes more natural over time.

- Positive affirmations.

Affirmation cards are a visual reminder to engage in positive self-reflection. They come in all topics; however, for the purpose of this section, I would encourage you to make or find some positive self-love affirmations! I keep mine on my desk at work and each day I flip to a new card. You can use the card as a guide for your day, a topic for journaling, or thoughts to ponder in meditation. Affirmation cards can be a powerful tool because we are fallible (which means we make mistakes) and as such we will forget to engage in healthy habits, even if we intended to! The cards serve as a visual cue for you to come back to the practice of mindful reflection and self-love.

I am sure you know that on some level, positive affirmations are useful tools to build your self-worth and self-esteem; however, I am also sure that there are times in which the statements are too much of a stretch for you. If the gap between your current mentality and the positive affirmation is too wide, you are likely to give up and avoid practicing. The answer to this conundrum is to add "what if". *What if* you believed them? You can add "what if" to the beginning of the affirmation as a bridge to cross the wide gap and move towards acceptance of the statement and consider the possibility that perhaps you are more than you think you are.

You may struggle to believe "I have the power to control my thoughts", especially if you struggle with anxiety and rumination. If it feels like Susie Sunshine is harassing you in reading that first affirmation, try reading it like this: *"What if I have the power to control my thoughts?"* Many people find that it will feel more realistic and believable in that format. It can make a huge difference in the choices you make because if there is a chance that you DO have power and control over your thoughts, you might be less likely to give into your next impulsive urge! A second example is the affirmation: "I am worthy of good things". If you are struggling with that idea, try stating internally *"what if I am worthy of good things?"* and let your day unfold from there without any self-sabotage.

o   Follow self-love and positive body image on social media.

It takes effort to unsubscribe/unfollow pages that might be damaging to you because they cause negative comparison thought, encourage problematic behavior, fixate on negatives, or otherwise bring you down and yet it is effort that I think you will be glad to have spent once you are finished.

If you are going to be scrolling on social media, then you need to be seeing the right messages! Be sure to follow pages, hashtags, and content that motivate you, encouraged self-love and generally put out content that energizes you! Whether your children are toddlers, teens or somewhere in-between, teaching them to set boundaries with where they invest their time and energy is a great life skill. Starting with social media is a great step towards altering how you (or they) spend their free time.

o   Take time each day to center yourself.

You love your children enough to help them feel confident and loved. I implore you to love yourself enough to help yourself feel confident and loved. You are deserving of your own energy just as much as they are. Taking time to center yourself can include taking a walk in the neighborhood each morning, enjoying a mug of tea outside, allowing yourself to close the door when you are in the bathroom, journaling, and praying. Spending time grounding yourself by engaging in a habit that centers you will allow you to be a less reactive parent as well!

What centers you?
_____
_____
_____
_____
_____

Self-Confidence:

Self-confidence is the degree to which you have faith in your own abilities. This includes everything from your own abilities to cook an edible meal (small stuff) to your abilities to raise a child from birth into a functional adult (big stuff).

If your self-confidence is lacking, I suggest you ask your child for a lesson in how to get it back. Kids are inherently confident people, they are much more likely to jump into social situations, try new activities, and brag about their accomplishments (even mediocre ones)! Your child also sees you as a superhero; if you fall into thinking that you do not have a talent, I challenge you to ask them what you are good at. One time when I walked into my daughter's preschool classroom, I was confused as the kids ran up to me and asked about my art. I didn't know what they were talking about, but the teacher filled me in on the fact that my daughter told them all that I am a "real artist"! I was so flattered because I dabble in art and very much enjoy it; however, never thought so much as to call myself a professional artist! Kids will stroke your ego for you until you can have faith in your own abilities!

Ask your child(ren) what you are good at and record their answers here:
_____
_____

_____
_____
_____
_____
_____

Ideas for Increasing Self-Confidence

o   Hone a skill or craft.

With choosing a skill or craft, I encourage you to look back at chapter one and pick something that you find enjoyable which may even connect to your personal values. Review the "building mastery" section of chapter four to remind yourself of this concept. I want you to bookmark the idea that getting good at something builds confidence. My next statement (before you go too far down the rabbit hole) is that very few people are born with pure untrained talent. Most people start with shaky legs, and it takes diligence and effort before they are running with the ease you see. Most people start with tutorials and practice over and over before they can produce a product independently. Most people have a series of "fails" before they start having a series of "wins".

What are your hobbies, talents, or areas that you can continue to build mastery in?
_____
_____
_____
_____
_____
_____
_____

o   Cherish your mistakes.

This might be my favorite suggestion and as a therapist I see it as a critical learning lesson for young people. Cherishing your mistakes has two parts. First, I urge you to be willing to take ownership of your mistakes with eyes open. Second, I encourage you to share the experience with others. The reality is that all people make mistakes and mistakes are very rarely a crisis; however, since very few people are doing step two, you probably have the shame-experience of feeling like the only fool in the world!

Think of this with the example of forgetting to pay a bill. Most adults that I know have forgotten to pay a bill in the last few years; however, no one is talking about it. As a result of this ongoing secrecy, teens get into negative financial situations after making honest mistakes and they are terrified to tell anyone (shame-experience) which perpetuates a decades long cycle of shame and debt! When I ask my teen clients what they think happens if you forget to pay your water bill or car payment, they universally jump to the worst-case scenario: water gets shut off, car gets repossessed, or they send you to collections. The reality is that none of those things happen unless you default on the payment for several months and ignore the company's efforts to contact you via letters, calls, and emails. I tell my teen clients that I forget to pay bills (that is step two) because I want to rewrite my own shame and help them avoid falling into the shame-cycle when they make mistakes!

o   Power posing.

Power posing is a fascinating psychological discovery about the power of the mind-body connection and your ability to cheat the system. Power posing was born in 2012 when researcher and psychologist Ann Cuddy, in partnership with Harvard, did studies on posturing and the effect on brain chemistry. It was found that having expansive postures (confident, superhero-esq posture) resulted in higher levels of testosterone and lower levels of cortisol. This brain chemistry shift resulted in more success in job interviews and increased participation and eye contact in the classroom setting. It is a great example of when "Fake it 'til you make it" actually works! Cuddy replicated the findings in a study of 2018 as well, finding that indeed your posture has a direct impact on your self-confidence. The simplest way to practice power posing is to find a private space and stand with a superhero pose for two minutes. It is that simple (Cuddy et al, 2018).

Can you identify any scenarios with parenting that you could benefit from increased confidence?

___

As an introvert, I can tell you that this skill is incredibly helpful before I interact with other parents at my kid's school or when they join a new sports team that requires me to introduce myself and mingle!

Take some time now to look up the TED talk or Youtube video of Ann Cuddy discussing power posing. What are your thoughts?

___

- Reflect on past accomplishments.

I like to encourage people to look forward; the past is the past and fixating on it can bring on feelings of depression and regret. There is truth; however, in the benefits of looking back with intention and purpose. Sometimes that means looking back to remember and grieve a lost loved one, sometimes it means looking back to evaluate patterns for problem solving purposes, and sometimes it means looking back to reflect on past successes as a reminder that you do have the ability to accomplish goals.

I encourage you to dedicate one page in your journal to listing out past successes. Ask yourself:

- When have I faced my fears?
- What is good feedback I have received in the past from friends, co-workers, bosses, and my children?
- What are some DIY projects I have completed on my own?
- What are some goals I have achieved in the past related to my finances, health, schedule, etc.
- Do I have any trophies or awards that provide physical proof of my accomplishments?
- What would other people say I have succeeded at?

_____
_____
_____
_____
_____
_____
_____
_____
_____
_____
_____
_____
_____
_____

- Manifest confidence when it is lacking.

Manifesting is a type of meditation in which you practice having thoughts of success and will them to happen. Manifesting alone does not produce outcomes with 100% success; however, manifesting is the internal mantra and dialogue in which you repeatedly tell yourself that you can, and you will succeed. With a mindset of empowerment, I believe you will be more likely to put action steps into place which increase the likelihood of success. Manifesting will silence your inner critic and allow you to imagine the success that you seek.

Manifesting generally sounds like: "I will stay calm with my kids today", "my boss will offer me a raise in the near future", "I will be physically healthy". When you allow yourself to confidently say and believe these thoughts, it will allow the inspiration and confidence required to make changes in your life to achieve the goals (such as deep breathing before engaging with your kids, improving your focus and productivity at work, and/or drinking more water and taking more steps each day).

You can use the "what if" technique with manifesting as well if you don't feel that you can be firm and absolute with saying things such as "I will stay calm today" – you can say "what if I stay calm today" instead.

Learning to love yourself will directly benefit your child. Learning to implement the strategies for loving and respecting yourself through action and the words you use will directly teach your child to do the same! As we know, little eyes are always watching and little ears are always listening, I want you to feel confident that you are speaking about yourself in ways you would like them to speak about themselves! I want them to see you take care of yourself physically, mentally, spiritually, financially, etc. so that they learn to do the same when they are older!

Questions to journal on:
1. After reading the definitions of self-worth, self-esteem, and self-love, which of the three do you think you struggle the most with?
2. What is one suggestion from this chapter that you are ready to

implement? How will you do that?
3. Why is it important to you that your child(ren) grow up to feel good about themselves?

6 WHERE AM I GOING WRONG?

"Success consists of going from failure to failure without loss of enthusiasm."
—Winston Churchill

Failure is a part of the change process; I implore you not to run away from it or hide in shame when it happens! Change is difficult, complex, and overwhelming at times. It is realistic and expected that you will encounter failure along the way if you are trying to change habits in your life. As Winston Churchill indicates in the above quote; success is born from failure. Knowing that this is the case can empower you to embrace the difficulties and press forward!

In a large-scale study on the dynamics of failure (and therefore success) from 2019, researchers Yin, Wang, Evans and Wang analyzed 776,721 grant applications submitted to the National Institutes of Health from 1985 to 2015. They found that those who succeeded and those who failed made similar amounts of attempts; persistence was not the key. The key to what led people to succeed in their goal was whether they stopped to evaluate what errors they were making and subsequently adjusted accordingly. The cliché *"work smarter, not harder"* is fifty percent true after all. Both the people who succeeded and the people who failed worked hard; the part that we must strive for is the *"work smarter"* part! This chapter will unpack what you might be missing that is leading to your undesired outcomes.

Complex Change

Learning how to assess failure and adjust your plan is the key to increasing your success of achieving desirable outcomes. I have found a visual reference referred to as the Lippit-Knoster Model for Managing Complex Change that will help illustrate the process (Villa & Thousand, 2000) and will help you find where you might miss the stepping stone to achieve the meaningful change that you want in life!

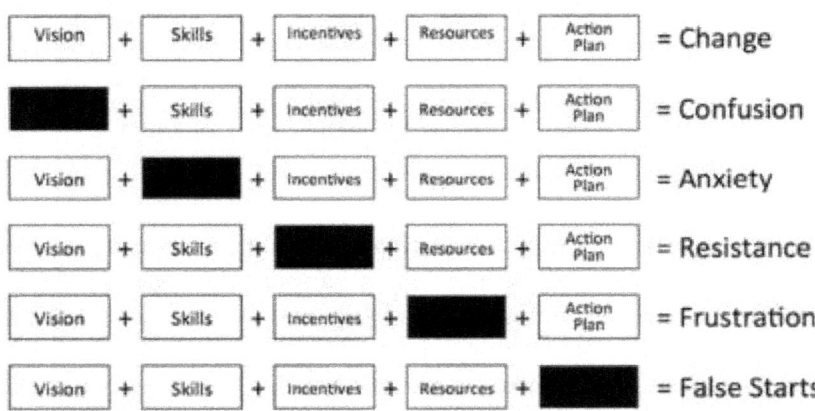

If you have picked up this book, then I know you want change. Change is the outcome of the top row; if you follow the equation provided, you are likely to experience change. The unfortunate reality for most working parents though, is that we desperately want to change; however, we run into roadblocks. We often end up getting confused and/or anxious, feeling resistant to the process and barriers we experience, frustrated by the process, or we end up preparing to change but never actually doing it! In walking through the grid, you can learn what steps you might be faltering at and explore ways to shore them up. Identifying your stumbling blocks is not meant to highlight your failure and bring on shame; rather, it opens the door to problem solving and lets in the light of hope. By defining and picking apart the key concepts within the model, you can find hope in your ability to move forward and persevere throughout the change process. By making these changes on a personal level, I believe you can and will improve your parenting outcomes as well!

What is something you would like to change?

_____
_____
_____
_____
_____
_____

Vision

Vision is what you want to see your life become. It is the goal you set for yourself. Your personal vision is an idealistic future that you are setting for yourself related to one facet of life. Your vision helps you to identify what to strive for and what you want to achieve. Having a vision will empower you to steer all relevant decisions toward achievement of the idealized future. This is important it will allow you to know when you have achieved your goal! Articulating your vision (both to yourself and to others) will help you feel motivated and will comfort your anxiety as without a vision you might feel like you are floating aimlessly through life.

A vision statement is generally short, sweet, and to the point. It is generally simple enough for anyone to read and understand; this is important for you as well because I do not want you to read it months later and forget what you meant by the words you used! Vision statements are not generally perfect the first time you try. Take time and be willing to edit it over the weeks to nail down what you really hope to achieve. It is critical that your vision statement is something that YOU want to achieve; not something that society or other people think you should achieve. I suggest considering a vision that will realistically take approximately one year to achieve (think chapter four's review of the "build mastery" skill). We need to set something that is achievable in a time frame that keeps us motivated AND that is realistic. Change does not happen overnight, and I see many people stumble with this…we all want the quick fix.

An ideal vision statement contains measurable components, a personal component that makes sense based on your circumstances, and how it will improve connection to others. As you can see in the complex change diagram, if you do not have clearly defined vision statement, you will end up with confusion! You are likely to jump on fad bandwagons (fitness, diets, trends, etc.) and you will lack direction overall in life. A vision statement is a necessary part of change!

As a parent it is important to have a vision statement for yourself as not to lose your sense of identity.

My vision statement is: *I will feel able to keep up with my kids and husband when hiking the National Parks and will live my life with minimal joint pain and exhaustion. I will be saying "yes" more than I say "no" as it relates to physical activities with those I love.* This vision statement promotes my identities as an individual, a wife and a mother. It speaks to my passion for the National Parks and my goal to pass on values of health, persistence, and family connectivity onto my children.

Take this space to work on a vision statement for yourself:

_____
_____
_____
_____
_____
_____
_____
_____
_____
_____
_____
_____
_____
_____
_____
_____
_____
_____
_____
_____

Skills

We are taught a lot of things in elementary school. I can sing the 50 United States in alphabetical order, I can tell you random facts about history and I can tell you about primary, secondary, and tertiary colors from the color wheel, but I am not sure that I learned the necessary life skills of problem solving, budgeting, or communication. It is not your fault if you are lacking in the skills needed to achieve your goal, but it is your responsibility to learn them now.

I love how normalized self-help books, blogs, and topics are in our world. If you feel that you need the skills associated with achieving goals, I encourage you to check out my first book <u>Adulting Well: Utilizing the Theories and Strategies of Dialectical Behavioral Therapy</u> for practical and relatable help in different areas of life. Coping skills, communication skills, and problem-solving skills are required to gain the confidence needed to tackle complex goals. Improving your skills can keep you out of the pit of anxious despair and prevent you from beating yourself up. There is not one magic skill; rather, you will have to continually assess and reassess where you are in life and alter your course accordingly.

My example on solving the problem related to lack of exercise skills needed to support my vision includes consulting with personal trainers every few years to refine my plan, having accountability buddies in my life to help remind me to get to the gym and eat well, and in seasons where my motivation is lacking, I find that attending fitness classes is helpful!

What skills do you need to hone in order to work toward your vision?

_____
_____
_____
_____
_____
_____
_____
_____

Incentives

Humans are animals. Animals can be trained. To be trained, animals need reinforcement. A reinforcer is anything that is likely to increase the odds of a behavior/action happening again. A positive reinforcer is something given that you want to receive (treat, item, kind words, sticker) and a negative reinforcer is the removal of something that you want removed (removal of an unpleasant task/chore, removal of discomfort, removal of guilt). The reinforcer can come from an external source such as an accountability partner, a spouse, a friend, or a paid professional or from within yourself. I suggest building both internal and external reinforcers into your change process.

I have noticed that we are quicker to jump to self-punishment instead of reinforcers. We think that it will help motivate us; however, research and your own experience continues to prove that idea WRONG. If beating yourself up with your words and actions helped, we would all be perfectly productive in our goals! Scientific research has shown again and again that punishment is the least effective method for changing behavior. If you would like to learn more on this, check out Karen Pryor's book Don't Shoot The Dog.

Without incentives animals/humans do not engage in behaviors that are difficult or cause discomfort. Without incentives, you will be resistant to change and can end up being resentful of the change! Resistance is not the desired outcome, change is.

I found that to reinforce myself for my goal of increasing and maintaining consistent physical exercise, I used a variety of reinforcers. I have a behavior chart in my journal in which I check off the days that I exercise. Having a definition is important! My definition of exercise was if I went to the gym, went on a hike or bike ride, or walked 7000 steps per day. As I found myself achieving the goal most days, I raised the bar and separated exercise from 7000 steps per day. I wanted 7000 steps to be my baseline and wanted to do physical exercise at least four times per week on top of that. My other incentives have included but are not limited to a new water bottle/workout clothes after hitting pre-defined goals, removal of guilt over skipping workouts, allowing myself to watch a show only after I exercise, certain "gym-only" playlists, encouragement from my friends, kids and husband, positive self-talk and self-encouragement, and noticing my gains such as improved energy and stamina. Please notice that there is not one answer, there will need to be a variety of reinforcers that come together for the benefit of incentivizing your success.

Identify incentives that might work for you? Initially, do not ignore any ideas.

_____
_____
_____
_____
_____
_____
_____
_____
_____

Resources

What in the world do we mean by resources? Resources are assets that can be pulled from by a person to function effectively. Without resources you will be very frustrated because you will not be able to achieve your goals! If your goal requires you to pay a fee, the needed resource is money. If your goal includes producing artwork, your resource would be the art supplies. If your goal includes making friends, your resources might include therapy to learn the anxiety management skills needed to overcome social anxiety.

Your resources are the items, funds, and/or people required to achieve the goal. I say required to highlight the fact that without the appropriate resources, you will not be able to achieve the goal! You can have a clear vision, great motivators, and amazing skills; but without the resources required, the goal will be intangible. Sometimes you might not have the ability to obtain the resources due to lack of money or opportunity. If this is the case you will need to problem solve, and/or choose another vision to work on initially. Berating yourself is not helpful.

The resources I used to achieve my health and fitness vision included: the money required for a Beachbody on Demand subscription for at home workouts as I have three kids and cannot always get to a gym, the money for a gym membership to Planet Fitness for days that I can get to the gym, weights and at home workout gear which I purchased used, workout clothing and a water bottle. Money was a resource needed for each step of the way. When money was tight, I skipped the Beachbody subscription and used free workouts on Youtube which was adequate; however, Wifi and a device were still needed resources. Time is also a needed resource, so I have had to sharpen my time management skills to make time.

What is the cost to you? What resources do you need to work on the change?

___
___
___
___
___
___
___
___
___
___
___
___
___
___
___
___
___
___
___
___
___
___
___
___
___
___
___
___
___
___

Action Plan

Your action plan needs to be a specific set of steps that attend to all logistical concerns you can think of. Within your action plan, you need to be able to define the where, what, when, how, and who of your goal. An action plan needs to be broken down into a simple, easy to follow set of guidelines and steps. This is where we break that lofty vision statement into a set of realistic and achievable steps. Your action plan likely needs to include:
- o The logistics of who, what, when, where, and how.
- o A list of people you can delegate tasks to (including childcare).
- o Your supporters and reinforcers and how/when you will use them.
- o A clearly defined outcome so that you will know whether you met your goal.
- o Unambiguously defined steps to take which will lead you to achieving identified tasks.

Without an action plan, you are likely to end up experiencing "false starts". You might hear yourself say *"I keep intending to change but never actually change"* or *"I've wanted this for years; I don't know why I can't get myself to do it"*. Without an action plan, the vision remains too vague and abstract.

Your action plan needs to take reality into account. It is not realistic that you will move from A to Z with ease. It is not likely that you will avoid the storms and unexpected barriers that life throws at us. Unexpected barriers often require skills and resources to overcome which will take your energy during that time. I do not tell you that to be discouraging; rather I am hoping to empower you to see the stumbles and detours as a part of the process rather than signs of personal failure. Full acceptance of the fact that there will be unpredicted upsets is required for you to allow yourself to develop and action plan that builds in the needed coping skills and reinforcers to move past the storms without giving up.

Examples of these pitfalls include but are certainly not limited to family crisis, financial difficulties, medical problems and injury, hormonal fluctuations, dips in motivation, temptations to engage in other activities. I encourage you to do introspection on what has gotten in the way of your success in the past and talk to peers about what gets in their way. Once you have your list of possible problems you can build coping skills and solutions into your action plan. It is not going to be possible to predict every stumbling block; however, working to anticipate some of them can keep you on track and get you back on track faster.

My action plan includes sitting down on Sunday evening to review my schedule (including my kids and husband's) and the weather. I find times that I can get to the gym (bearing in mind that I need a two-hour window at minimum to be able to drive to and from the gym, workout, shower and then do my hair and make-up for the next part of my day. If I have a shorter window, I often do go to the gym still but have a plan to only do weights and to try not to sweat since I will not have time for the shower. The weather comes into play because our family looks for a few "pick days" each week to engage in outdoor activities which count as exercise: hiking, biking, swimming. My action plan for the night before includes planning what I am going to wear at the gym, whether I need to take it to work with me, and planning food so that I have the energy to go. My action plan includes communicating the proposed schedule to my husband so that he can let me know if he sees any barriers. I have also noticed historically that I had a habit of driving to the gym but sitting in my car and scrolling social media before I go in (thus wasting my resource of time). I have addressed that by making social media an incentive: if I work hard at the gym, I allow myself down time on the stationary bike to cool down and scroll.

I fully believe that you can do this, parenting is no longer a valid excuse for not living the life you want. I believe you can make meaningful change. This complex problem-solving model can help guide you and help you to identify stumbling blocks. I encourage you to take some time to journal on the points mentioned here. You may need to reread this chapter to fully take it in so that you can make the changes that you want to see in your life!

What steps are in your action plan?
_____
_____
_____
_____
_____

Questions to journal on:

1. What do you think about the research that indicates a need to keep assessing and changing our strategy when trying to change?
2. Do you feel invigorated by the complex change model or fearful of it?
3. Which step do you think you had faltered at in the past?

7 TOOLS FOR SUCCESS

"Success is the sum of small efforts - repeated day in and day out." -- Robert Collier

Social media is unavoidable in the twenty-first century. I encourage you to look at how you use various social media platforms for mental health instead of mental anguish. I would like to share this Native American parable with you:

An old Cherokee is teaching his grandson about life. "A fight is going on inside me," he said to the boy. "It is a terrible fight, and it is between two wolves. One is evil – he is anger, envy, sorrow, regret, greed, arrogance, self-pity, guilt, resentment, inferiority, lies, false pride, superiority, and ego."

He continued, "The other is good – he is joy, peace, love, hope, serenity, humility, kindness, benevolence, empathy, generosity, truth, compassion, and faith. The same fight is going on inside you – and inside every other person, too."

The grandson thought about it for a minute and then asked his grandfather, "Which wolf will win?"

The old Cherokee simply replied, "The one you feed."

Which wolf do you feed? Which one do you spend more time nurturing?

_____
_____
_____
_____
_____
_____
_____
_____
_____
_____
_____
_____
_____
_____
_____
_____

Friendships

Friendships are a necessary part of life and regardless of how you feel about whether you want new friends, I am telling you that it is necessary. As friendships take time to evolve, they can also take time before we realize they have imploded. Many blogs and vlogs exist on ending romantic relationships, but what about friendships? Often, our friendships are longer and, in some ways, more complicated. Our hope is that we have friendships that are psychologically safe, allow us to feel supported and accepted, and promotes our growth.

A healthy friendship is one that:

- Allows you to make your own choices.
- Respects your opinions that might be different than their own.
- Does not impede your ability to achieve your own goals.
- Encourages you to prioritize self-care.
- They are proud of your successes.
- They promote your growth in any/all arenas (spiritually, physically, mentally, academically, etc.)

Who are your healthy friends? What do you enjoy the most about their friendship?

_____
_____
_____
_____
_____
_____
_____
_____
_____
_____
_____
_____
_____
_____
_____
_____

Why might you want to end an unhealthy relationship? The simplest and most clear-cut answer happens when there is a breach of trust: theft, infidelity involving the friend, and someone deemed "off limits" or any sort of abuse from the friend towards yourself. The reality is that most of the time, it is not that clear-cut; rather, it is a slow erosion over time that leaves you questioning how you got to this point and what can/should be done about it. With slow erosion the friendship drifts apart over months or years. You might find that you no longer feel invigorated when spending time together, you leave feeling badly about yourself, you feel shamed for your choices or interests when with the person, or you simply feel that spending time with that person just doesn't cross your mind as much anymore. I believe a relationship turns from distant to toxic when the person actively works against the healthy attributes listed in the bullet points above. Signs of a toxic friendship are:

- They tell you who you can and cannot spend time with.
- They make fun of your interests and/or hobbies and/or put

you down.
- They refuse to have discussions about differences; rather they adopt a "my way or the highway" stance that shuts down a conversation and leaves you feeling as though you are walking on eggshells.
- They ignore your requests for self-care (such as a night in, desires to distance yourself from other toxic people, plans to reduce your alcohol consumption, etc.)
- They tease you about goals that you set in ways that aren't playful or loving.
- They "one up" you and cause you to dread bringing up any of your successes because you have learned that they will take over the conversation and instead of being happy for you, they make it about themselves.
- They never reach out to you or initiate contact.

Does that list bring any people to mind? What parts of the friendships you have are unhealthy?

_____
_____
_____
_____
_____
_____
_____
_____

With those factors being explained, hopefully you can see the clear difference between a friendship that builds you up and one that holds you back or actively tears you down.

You may have urges to "ghost" the person (meaning just disappear from their life); however, I urge you not to do that. Learning to speak up for yourself is a huge and necessary life task. Modeling this for your children will provide them with a great structure for their own relationships as well! I encourage you to let the friend know what has been bothering you (in factual, non-blaming ways) and let them know that you plan to distance yourself to work on your own needs. This might sound like you saying:

"Rob, I've noticed that when we spend time together, I fall into some unhealthy thinking patterns and I end up feeling really alone since we've grown in different directions (insert example), I'm going to take a few weeks to see if I can sort out my thoughts on the topic. I hope you can understand my need for space" or *"Sara, the last few times we have hang out, I have had my feelings hurt by the comments you have made about people who want to be sober, and you keep bringing wine over even though I've told you that I quit drinking. I need to stop having you over to my house because of this"*.

Try to stick to "I" statements, such as *"I feel, I notice, I've been experiencing"* etc. instead of *"you"* statements which tend to make the other person defensive. It is possible that the friend might not take this news very well; however, as you were already considering "ghosting" them, I think the skill and confidence you will gain from speaking up is worth it! If we think back to who you want your child(ren) to become, I will bet confident, assertive, and honest are on the list of attributes you want for them. Since they are always watching, you can use these difficult scenarios as teaching moments.

What is the cost of ending a toxic relationship?

- Sadness and grieving.
- Boredom.
- Anxiety.
- Vulnerability when trying to meet new people.
- Hypervigilance in new relationships.
- Second guessing yourself.

What is gained when a toxic relationship ends:

- Independence.
- Freedom to do/say/wear the things your friend made you feel shame about wanting to do/say/wear.
- Time for yourself.
- A healthier sense of self.
- More energy to be around and engage with your kids.

When ending a toxic relationship of any type, it is crucial that you take time to rebuild your sense of self and self-worth. You may have strong urges to distract yourself away from the negative feelings you are feeling; but you need to take the time to heal. This means that you take time for your hobbies and interests, you spend time with people that build you up and you spend some time with yourself – rediscovering who you are and want to be!

What fears do you have about confronting the unhealthy parts of your current friendships?

_____
_____
_____
_____
_____
_____
_____
_____
_____
_____
_____
_____
_____
_____
_____
_____
_____
_____
_____
_____

Friendships are critical and I chose to go in depth on this topic because your friendships are a key place to find accountability. We do not exist in a vacuum; people need social interaction to survive! This is a well-known fact in human development. What also seems true; however, is that we need other humans to encourage us! Have you ever noticed how even with high levels of motivation and anticipation about starting something or going somewhere new, when it comes down to doing it you are prone to coming up with a lot of excuses? Having an accountability partner is a technique that fitness gurus cite over and over in terms of how to get into a new workout routine and stay there! Alcoholics Anonymous has built in the same concept by urging members to get a sponsor. Diet programs often have check in buddies or online communities as well.

An accountability partner is someone who will go with/participate with/check-in with you regarding the new behavior you are working on increasing or decreasing. It is even better if they are also working toward the same goal.

Who can be your accountability buddy?

_____
_____
_____
_____
_____
_____
_____
_____
_____
_____

What if you do not have enough friends? Making friends as an adult can seem overwhelming and it certainly takes longer than it did in high school. To start, it is recommended that you begin frequenting locations that align with the interests and values that you identified in chapter one. This might mean that you frequent the same coffee shop, the same craft store, the same farmer's market, or possibly the same gym. If you put effort into going at around the same time and one the same day, you will become a "regular" and you will start recognizing familiar faces, and they will recognize you! At that point you can begin small talk and move towards a more active connection. Support groups are another win-win for meeting people and increasing accountability. It's great when they are in person, many people find it's easier to connect in that format; but I would encourage you to try them out either way.

Technology

But what should you do if you don't have a network of friends that can or wants to provide accountability? You can go high tech! Technology is at our fingertips and on our wrists all the time, so I propose that you start making it work for you! I have seen some great habit tracking apps and I know many people who swear by their smart watch or fitness tracking devices. I know this chapter isn't only about fitness, I share it as a clear example. Luckily there are apps for almost every habit you could want to work on (sobriety, gratitude journaling, washing your face, watering your plants, tracking your finances) and they all allow you to subscribe to push-notifications to keep you motivated.

As a tool, social media sites can be used for both good and evil. You can subscribe to blogs and pages that fixate on negativity, make you feel worse, join in your pity party, highlight the negative events in the world, etc. or you can subscribe to those that are positive, encouraging and motivating. On all social networking sites, the users, and topics that you search, subscribe to, and follow are up to you. Try following inspiration, funny pictures, cute animals, users that make a point of being encouraging, and/or appropriate family members. A big no-no here is following triggering topics, users that bring you down, encourage behavior(s) that you are trying to stop doing, highly judgmental users, and/or topics that normalize behavior(s) you do not want to continue. If a user or topic makes your conscious put up a red flag or if it is something you feel ashamed to follow, remove it!!

One benefit of the pandemic that hit our world in 2020 is that it took all industries and put them online. Initially, we all struggled with screen fatigue; however, now that we are settling into this "new normal", I can see the benefit of increased access to support for all issues. You no longer need to live in a big city to access resources; WIFI opens a new world of opportunities! Support groups are also now offered on-line which grants you access to a wide range of support topics that may not have been previously offered in your region.

What are some healthy ways you can use technology to help you remain accountable and stay motivated?

_____
_____
_____
_____
_____
_____
_____
_____

In what way are you using technology that are not helpful?

_____
_____
_____
_____
_____
_____
_____
_____
_____

Journaling

Journaling has evolved and is not just for middle school girls anymore! Journaling is simply writing down your thoughts and feelings to understand them more clearly. Journaling can give you increased insight and discover patterns in your own behaviors. With this insight, you will feel more in control of your emotions and behaviors. Increasing insight is like driving around with your bright headlights on at night on a country road – you will be able to see dangers sooner and adjust course before engaging in problematic habits.

Consider using a journal as a tool to explore your ideas, make plans for yourself and document your successes! Journaling does not need to have any negative stigma attached to it. If you are interested, you can try different types of journaling:

1. Bullet journaling –

Bullet journaling tends to appeal to those who enjoy organization and like to see the data of their life. Bullet journaling can motivate you to keep up with difficult habits by tracking the "streak" over time. Bullet journaling is generally done using grid paper and a variety of charts and doodles with the goal of keeping track of your behaviors. There are great premade bullet journal spreads for sale, and you can also create your own by searching for bullet journal blogs or videos online and engaging your creative nature!

2. Daily recording –

A daily recording journal is will feel more like a traditional diary. The goal is that you take time each day to reflect. Whether you sit down with your morning coffee, taking a break midday to reflect or use it as a way to wrap up your evenings is up to you, and I suggest you experiment with different time frames to find which set-up is best of you.

3. Behavior charts –

Behavior charts are just like when you were a child! The reality is that we are all animals and animals require rewards and reinforcement to learn and sustain new habits. By giving yourself a star or smiley face each time you succeed, you are acknowledging your own efforts and increase the likelihood that you will continue!

4. Art Journaling –

Art journaling is generally done in a sketch book. It is where you make a sketch, collage, or doodle each day to capture something about your day. Art journaling accesses the creative part of your brain and can be very enjoyable, assuming you are willing to set your judgments about your artistic talent aside and allow the process to unfold naturally.

5. Self- Inquiry Journaling –

Self- inquiry is the process of questioning yourself and finding potential hidden hot spots of resistance or defensiveness that prohibit your growth. Personal growth can flourish with this type of journaling as you will dig deeply into your inner thoughts in a narrative type of journaling, being fully honest with yourself. As you have already set goals for yourself related to values, self-inquiry requires you to evaluate what barriers you are running into. It is also a great way to celebrate the successes you have experienced in overcoming those barriers. A goal would be that you spend time writing a few times per week or daily and be willing to be completely honest with yourself.

All forms of journaling serve the same purpose: to help you reflect on your day and explore patterns. There is no need to commit to one form exclusively. Your journal is your friend, it should be a place you can turn to record your wins and your losses, your highs and your lows, your dreams and your fears. You can vision cast a future version of yourself and explore the risks and rewards of plans you are considering enacting. Exploring future and ideas on paper is safer than jumping feet-first into a scenario blindly, unaware of likely risks.

Questions to journal on:

1. What habits that this book has taught you could you use to feed the right wolf?
2. Are you willing to speak up about your needs in your friendships? What is something you could say to a friend who is unintentionally making things harder for you?
3. Which type of journaling do you feel more interested in trying?

_____
_____
_____
_____
_____
_____
_____
_____
_____
_____
_____
_____
_____
_____
_____
_____
_____
_____
_____
_____

8 MAKING THE CHANGE YOU DESERVE

"Motivation is what gets you started. Habit is what keeps you going." --Jim Ryun

Most people I talk to about the mental health ideas presented in this book DO agree with the suggestions (healthy diet, exercise, early to bed, have time with friends, etc.). Most people can also see that the strategies are "low hanging fruit" in that they are readily available and do not generally cost a lot of money; and yet we avoid them like the plague! The problem is that while we know what to do, we struggle to implement the suggestions. There is not an intelligence issue, there is a motivation and consistency problem.

How do you get yourself to start a new habit? How do you get yourself to change the expectations you have for your kids? How do you make time for yourself as a parent?

_____
_____
_____
_____
_____
_____
_____

There are clear steps that a person needs to take in order to make and sustain change. If you can implement these steps, you will move forward and gain the momentum needed to make changes with your habitual behaviors. Having a plan always makes the journey more realistic!

1. Identify the problem. This is easier said than done. Make sure that the problem is a YOU problem. (For example, saying "my spouse doesn't let me have time to myself" is not a you problem. "I have been fearful about asserting my needs" is a *you* problem.) If we are going to address something, it needs to be something in your control to address. You cannot make someone else do something. You CAN work on your communication skills.

   What is a simple "you" problem to practice on?

2. Identify the gap between the problem and the desired outcome. What new habit or skill do I think will fix it? (I.e.: I am not setting aside time for my goals; I continue to schedule things for my kids and not myself; I need to learn different communication skills)

   What is the gap or skill you need to work on with your example?

   _____
   _____
   _____
   _____
   _____
   _____
   _____
   _____
   _____
   _____

3. Get some wind in those sails. I find that research and reinforcement are key with this step. You already have the emotional urge for change; now you need to see the numbers, statistics and hear the logical arguments on why other people believe in the habit and what they are doing to achieve it. You need to access ideas on how to grow and strengthen the skills needed and ways to learn them. This information is reinforcing to your desire for change and is critical as we learned in chapter seven within the complex change model. This includes watching YouTube videos, reading blogs, research studies and books, and talking to professionals. You may need to do some research on time management. You are already doing research on change by reading this book!

   Where can you turn for research and reinforcement?

   _____
   _____
   _____

_____
_____
_____
_____
_____
_____
_____
_____

4. Take your time. I want you to ponder this change…a lot. New Year's Resolutions do not tend to last, and one reason is because people try to jump into change impulsively and they do not take the time needed to really convince themselves to invest in the long term. I want you to feel like you fully understand why this change would be beneficial. Pondering a topic is helpful in setting your vision statement and exploring what is likely to get in the way. As a parent, I think parenting pride can be helpful. I want you to remind yourself how proud you will feel if you model and instill healthy values and habits in your kids. This energy can help you push forward on the days when you *"don't wanna"*. I want you to be able to defend the decision and hopefully recruit friends to join you in the process!

   What are some of the reasons you would like to make the change you indicated in steps one and two?

   _____
   _____
   _____
   _____
   _____
   _____
   _____
   _____
   _____

5. Set SMALL Goals. If it were easy to make radical lifestyle changes…we would all do it! Set SMALL goals (and larger goals) and then start taking steps toward the small goals first. The successes of your small steps become self-reinforcing, and you will find yourself taking larger steps than planned. You will gain more steam as you go along, a snowball effect over time.

   How many small steps can you identify in making the change you identified?

   _____
   _____
   _____
   _____
   _____
   _____
   _____
   _____
   _____
   _____

6. Plan to fail. You read that correctly, plan for things to go wrong. Often, we can get through steps one through five and we start experiencing successes which feels so good! The problem we run into is that we do not have a plan for the inevitable bumps in the road. For example, if you made a workout plan and you have been sticking to it for over a month, but then you get sick and must take a week off you may find yourself having urges to then give up because you lost your motivation. I want you to plan to experience failure and use self-encouragement and positive self-talk to remind yourself that it is normal to have set-backs. Set-backs do not equate to failure and are not a valid reason for giving up.

   What are some reasonable scenarios that might cause you to stumble on your journey? What are effective choices to make when they happen?

   _____

_____
_____
_____
_____
_____
_____
_____
_____

Breaking old patterns and making sustainable change will require you to keep with it an allow for the natural ebb and flow of motivation and progress. If you realize you are back sliding, go back to one of the lower steps and re-start there. If your child tried learning a new task, I think you would be encouraging. Use that same dialogue toward yourself because you are worth it!

Mindfulness

Mindfulness is the practice of focusing your attention on the present moment, without judgment or pressure. Mindfulness offers you complete psychological freedom from stress, worrying, racing thoughts, and anger. That may sound farfetched; however, with practice it is quite realistic. Mindfulness means that whatever the task is that you are doing, you are fully present doing it (mentally and physically). If you are brushing your teeth you are mentally planning your day, replaying an argument, trying to get your children motivated, and walking around your house, then you are suffering! By mindfully brushing your teeth (standing still, feeling the sensations, and allowing your mind to focus only on the task at hand) you will free yourself from the stress and suffering described above.

What are your initial thoughts about mindfulness?

_____
_____
_____
_____

_____
_____
_____
_____

As a parent mindfulness can be a super-power that you always have at your disposal! When parenting, this can be useful when:

- Playing with your child without multitasking
- Allowing your brain to settle while doing one chore at a time
- Not texting and driving
- Being fully present at doctor appointments and school meetings to take in all the information
- Being able to find one moment of joy in each day and take a mental photograph of it

Do you struggle to be fully present with your child(ren)?

_____
_____
_____
_____
_____
_____
_____
_____

Mindfulness is not only a hot topic in our culture today; it is a fantastic tool that anyone can utilize to gain immeasurable benefits. Many people equate mindfulness to meditation. This is accurate and inaccurate at the same time. Mindfulness is a large umbrella concept; meditation does fall under the umbrella; however so do many other techniques. Mindfulness is merely choosing to focus all your attention on one thing, one task, or one thought.

Under the mindfulness umbrella, there are two main techniques:

1. Focusing your attention ON something or a task.

2. Clearing your mind.

Frequent feedback that I get is that the first type of mindfulness is easier. In our culture, focusing on something is much more acceptable and thus feels more natural than focusing on nothing. There is a judgment that focusing on something is still accomplishing something, while clearing your mind is a "waste of time".

Focusing on "something" can take almost any form: purposeful conversations with eye contact and no cell phones, choosing to read a book with limited distractions, painting, doing a puzzle, breathing techniques, body scan, yoga, fully throwing yourself into a sport or exercise etc. The goal is that you control your attention as opposed to blowing through the breeze at its mercy. When being mindful, you may notice distracting thoughts or urges; however, you choose to let them pass.

Clearing your mind may indeed be more difficult; however, the benefits are life changing. What I hear most often is that it's weird or the people don't "know how" to do it. Clearing you mind can happen in many forms. Zen mindfulness suggests sitting upright and comfortable in a meditation position. The only goal is to sit upright and still. Thoughts will rise and fall; we don't judge or cling to them if possible. Sitting periods can be anywhere from 60 seconds to hours at a time. There are of course other ways to meditate: prayer, reciting mantras, contemplating an issue, chanting, listening to classical or calming music, etc.

I encourage you to buy into mindfulness and practice diligently because it works! I will admit I was a skeptic at first. I thought people would make fun of me or judge me (and perhaps they do…). I didn't think I could "make time" …I was too busy! I have kids! I had all the excuses and many of them were completely valid. I began practicing as to not be a hypocrite as a mental health professional. The benefits I experienced are right in line with the numerous studies out there and included elevated mood, mental clarity, improved ability to problem solve, increased feeling of connection, increased wisdom, improved productivity, optimism, decreased physical pain, improved sleep and increased confidence to name a few.

I urge you to give it a try. Start with stopping several times per day to intentionally focus your attention on the task at hand. If you are walking, walk. Feel the knee swing through, the weight transfer from foot to foot, and stop ruminating. If you are working, work. Stop multi-tasking, pay attention to the ink on the paper, to your fingers on the keyboard, to the voice on the phone. If you are watching TV, watch TV. Stop eating, stop folding laundry, put your phone down and just watch TV. It gets easier with time. Once you feel confident in your ability to control your attention in those ways, begin several times per day to stop and breathe. Just stop what you are doing and take 10 deep, slow breaths. Center yourself, and then carry on with the task at hand. After you feel capable in the breathing exercises, it is time for you to intentionally choose to block out time in your day to practice a formal sitting meditation practice. Whether 5 minutes or 50 minutes, just take time to sit and be still. You can use apps, guided meditation that are easily found online or use your own process.

Building your mastery in mindfulness will help you change habits and achieve a more peaceful household. You do not have anything to lose!

Questions to journal on:

1. What is one habit that you would like to begin or end?
2. What stops you from taking a step toward your goals?
3. What is your initial reaction to mindfulness as a practice?

_____
_____
_____
_____
_____
_____
_____
_____
_____
_____
_____
_____
_____
_____

9 DON'T LET IT GO, LET IT BE

"...and when the night is cloudy there is still a light that shines on me, shinin' until tomorrow, let it be" —The Beatles

"I will not whisper these words of wisdom; I will shout them for all to hear: let it be! Our culture tends to be quick to tell overwhelmed persons to "let it go"; however, I believe that advice oversimplifies a complex process. I propose that you are a little less like Elsa and a little more like the Beatles.

"Let it go" insinuates that the choice to accept a difficult fact or set of circumstances is a one-and-done, simple one-time act. "Let it go" leads people to feel like they are failures if they struggle to move past a difficult fact of their life.

How do you feel when someone suggests that you "let it go"?

_____
_____
_____
_____
_____
_____
_____

Acceptance

Parenting requires more acceptance than I could have ever imagined. Parenting causes you to feel every emotion with more intensity than you have ever felt the emotion before or even thought possible. Love is more fierce, anger is more intense, anxiety is scarier, sadness is deeper, and joy is amplified.

I would venture to say that acceptance, as a skill, is one of the most difficult concepts to practice. As a therapist, it can take months (or years) to help someone find their willingness to work on acceptance. It requires active practice over time to master. Acceptance is not a concept that one grasps overnight.

What are your initial thoughts about accepting life circumstances that are out of your control?

_____
_____
_____
_____
_____
_____
_____
_____
_____
_____

Acceptance is NOT:

- Agreeing with the situation.
- Loving the situation.
- Hoping that the situation happens again.
- Approving of the situation.
- Resigning yourself to the facts and letting them continue to happen (if they are against your goals).

To put this in the context of parenting, reflect on these examples:

- Your child has a toileting accident.

- Your child lies to you.
- Your child failed an academic assignment.
- Your child has a new diagnosis.
- Your child is vomiting, and you cannot go to work.

If we apply the idea of acceptance, we recognize that the circumstance is indeed happening (or has happened) and that it cannot be changed. History cannot be rewritten. Acceptance means you want to stop fighting against the facts as they have occurred and make a conscious choice to let it be. Let the anger be, let the fear be, notice it and put it down as if it were a knick-knack that you can choose whether to hold in your hands. Let it be and realize that you have several choices in front of you. The power to stop carrying the negative emotion and instead to step into the freedom of choice is liberating!

Acceptance is crucial to having a life you enjoy because it offers freedom from suffering by acknowledging what is, identifying where you have a choice, and therefore turning suffering into pain you can endure (and often problem solve). In many ways, once you learn to apply acceptance within the context of parenting, it can be your best friend! As stated above, acceptance does not require you to approve of or like the situation; rather, it requires you to wake up to the fact that at present, you cannot change the fact of the issue and that you want to stop being angry about it.

What benefits would you have if you accepted the examples above, instead of fighting against reality?

_____
_____
_____
_____
_____
_____
_____
_____
_____

Acceptance requires a lot of practice; it is not a concept that one grasps overnight. The idea behind acceptance can be generalized in the classic Serenity Prayer:

"Grant me the serenity to accept the things I cannot change, the courage to change the things I can, and the wisdom to know the difference."

This might be a helpful concept post up where you will see it regularly!

If you are still struggling with this idea, note that you always have four choices in every situation you face. These choices are pulled from Dialectical Behavioral Therapy (Linehan, 1993). Realizing that you always have four choices can help you stay out of the negative pit of "I have to...", "they always...", "I never have time to...", etc. If you fall into that pit, you might as well invite your neighborhood over for a pity party. Your four choices that can highlight your options, increase acceptance, and decrease negativity are:

1. Solve the problem.

If you can, often this is the easiest choice, and we overlook it. Think about the example of the toileting accident. You can solve this problem by cleaning up the child and the mess, redressing the child and moving on with your day. There is no need to drag the frustration of the accident with you for the remainder of your day.

If you want to use this strategy for solving the problem of a child failing an academic assignment you would have to let your anger, sadness and fear be and look at the problem objectively. We know that yelling at the child does not work. Shaming the child for the grade does not work. Generally, the child has already yelled at and shamed themselves. Solving the problem involves having a calm and loving conversation with them about what they think led to the low grade (such as lack of studying, the child not comprehending the material, or external factors like the child having a headache during the process). Solving the problem could be devising a study plan, hiring a tutor, or discussing the need for an intervention plan with the school for frequent headaches.

Can you think of any situations that you could work to solve, instead of staying angry, sad, or anxious?

_____
_____
_____
_____
_____
_____
_____
_____
_____
_____

2. Change your thinking/perception of the problem.

It is not easy to change how you are interpreting a situation. When a child lies to you, you are likely to have a "gut reaction" that leads you to have a quick emotion. "How dare they!" leads to anger. If you do not want to stay angry and continue to have power struggles with your child, we can work on acceptance by choosing to have a different perception of the problem. Lying is a developmentally and age-appropriate action for elementary school and middle school children. Often, they lie because they want to please you. They do not want you to know that they made a mistake. Remembering this interpretation can lead you to have more compassion, while still working to address the lying. Older youth tend to lie to avoid punishment. We all do this (think about what you might say if a police officer asks you if you knew you were speeding or if a boss asks why, you were late). We can address the lying without the anger if we change our interpretation.

What can you work on changing your perception of as it relates to your child's behavior?

_____
_____
_____
_____
_____
_____
_____

_____
_____

3. Tolerate the problem.

If we are being honest, many of us make the choice to stay frustrated or anxious because we are making the choice to tolerate the problem instead of working to problem solve and change our responses. Tolerating the problem is the mental equivalent of refusing to remove a pebble from your shoe; you can still walk, but each step gets more irritating to you. You may find that you are tolerating your child's behaviors such as not cleaning up after themselves instead of working on holding them accountable for their own messes. Making change can cause increased stress in the short-term but helps resolve the issue in the long-term. Tolerating the problem is the opposite: it helps us to avoid stress in the short term; however, we build resentment in the long-term and this damages relationships.

In what areas are you tolerating something that needs to be changed? Why do you think you are avoiding the change that needs to happen?

_____
_____
_____
_____
_____
_____
_____
_____
_____

4. Stay miserable and/or make it worse.

It is a widely accepted fact that parenting is exhausting. I believe that parenting fatigue is why we give into tantrums, allow our kids to get things we do not want them to have (electronics), and make other concessions that go against our best judgment. In making those concessions, we are choosing to stay miserable (and often to make things worse). When you are sick and tired of being sick and tired, you will be open to using the strategies in chapter eight to make changes in your parenting style and work toward the long-term goals, rather than giving into short-term demands and urges.

What are some examples of you choosing to stay miserable as it relates to parenting?

_____
_____
_____
_____
_____
_____
_____
_____
_____

In parenting, there will be circumstances that occur that you cannot directly change such as your child's medical situation, your child's ability to comprehend academic concepts with ease or difficulty, other kids offending your child, the rules of their school/sports/programs, etc. There will also be circumstances that you can change or shape: generally related to our behaviors which influence our emotions and thoughts

I hope that this chapter helps you to determine what is in your control and what is out of your control. Once you have a good grasp on that, you can take the appropriate action (either accept or change) to move forward instead of staying stuck. I believe acceptance is so difficult because as a culture, we are pushed to do things faster, bigger, stronger at every turn. We live in a world that wants more, more, more, thus giving the message that everything IS within our control. This leads to a very anxious society.

Acceptance requires clarity, the ability to discern what is legitimately in and out of our control. Acceptance is not to say that you will never change, it is not to say that you approve of the situation, and it is not to say that you like the situation. Acceptance is to say that you recognize that you no longer want to suffer as a result of fighting reality.

Let me give you a few examples:

Example 1: You were bullied in high school, and you continue to re-live it, dredge up the memories, look the offenders up on social media thus torturing yourself with the related thoughts.

Acceptance would mean recognizing that you are continuing to keep those memories alive and active in your mind (this is not to say the actual bullying is your fault or that it is something you shouldn't feel angry about), thus increasing your own suffering. Acceptance looks like: admitting what happened and really allowing yourself to feel sad for your high school self. You may need to disable your social media accounts as you are no longer going to allow those memories to rule your behaviors.

Example 2: You made poor financial choices in the past that have left you with debt and poor credit

Acceptance means that you recognize that you own your past choices and get honest with yourself about their present implications. Often when people are fighting the reality of their debt, they continue to spend excessively and put more and more on lines of credit. Acceptance would challenge you to live as if you believed you were capable of financial control (have a budget, pay more than minimum balance, etc.). Radical acceptance means you are going to change your internal self-talk and cease beating yourself up about past choices as they cannot be changed!

Once you practice acceptance on smaller things: gas prices going up, weather, your paycheck size… then (and only then) you can begin practicing acceptance on more difficult topics.

Questions to journal on:

1. How do you feel about acceptance after reading the chapter and examples?
2. Are you able to see how your refusal to accept your child's behaviors can lead to power struggles?
3. What are some small things you can practice accepting?

10 THE ELEPHANT IN THE ROOM

"You can focus on the things that are barriers or you can focus on scaling the wall or redefining the problem" —Tim Cook

Just as I suggested in chapter eight, when making change, we need to address the problems and barriers we may face. We must plan for failure in order to increase the odds of sustained change. I spoke with countless parents in writing this book and asked them to define what barriers they faced in meeting their own goals as a parent. This chapter will tackle their reported barriers.

There are a few barriers reported by working parents are that we have not yet covered are marital expectations, overextending yourself, and overcommitment.

What barriers to success are you struggling the most with?

_____
_____
_____
_____
_____
_____
_____

Marital expectations

Prior to having children, your marriage, and relationships likely looked very different than they are now. When you got married or started your relationship, it is reasonable to assume that you spoke with your partner about how things would work for your family if/when you decided to have children. You likely discussed division of labor, who would take off work when kids had appointments or needs, how you would discipline, and how you would structure your family. All of these discussions were idealistic at best because you could not know the temperament or needs of your future children, you could not predict your own physical and mental health, and you could not predict your current employment variables.

When reality hits, we must go back to the topic of acceptance. You and your partner will need to decide which of the four strategies you want to employ to cope with the unexpected circumstances surrounding:

- Your child's health and appointments
- Your own health an appointments
- Fatigue
- Household chores and maintenance
- Childcare
- Financial stresses
- Intimacy
- Workplace stresses and needs
- Your social life
- Your child's social life
- Your child's academic needs
- Your child's activities
- Your own educational and vocational plans
- All of the above factors as they relate to your partner and/or other children you may have

Change is inevitable; however, that does not mean that it occurs without stress. Many of the above factors may have been discussed; however, we often underestimate the cost that each will place on the family.

Now that reality is in full swing, you and your partner will need to reevaluate, without judgment, the facts of your circumstances. This may mean that preconceived gender roles are challenged, predetermined family structures need to change, boundaries and roles may need to be redefined.

Reflect on the list from the previous page and make a list of the circumstances in your family that are causing the most conflict (internally or externally) for you.

_____
_____
_____
_____
_____
_____
_____
_____
_____
_____
_____
_____
_____
_____

I suggest that you and your partner schedule a weekly meeting to discuss these issues. During that meeting, both parties will need to come to the table without anger or stubbornness to hear one another's needs. Creative problem solving can only occur if each person is willing to relinquish control and challenge their own belief system.

Initially, this meeting will feel overwhelming as there are many things to discuss. If the meeting time is kept sacred and prioritized, the list will become shorter and more manageable.

During this weekly meeting, I suggest you both come prepared with your planner/agenda, budget, to-do list, journal, and wallet. This is a great time to discuss the schedule for the week and be sure all bases are covered (no one wants to leave a kid waiting at school because both parents assume someone else is picking them up!). You can discuss the budget and pay any random bills that showed up that week (I'm looking at you picture day, walk-a-thon, and field trip permission slips). You can evaluate how the current division of labor is feeling and if adjustments need to be made.

When can you and your partner make time for this weekly meeting? Is that time ideal for both people? Is it likely to be a time where each person can focus?

_____
_____
_____
_____
_____
_____
_____
_____
_____

What worries do you have about scheduling a weekly meeting?

_____
_____
_____
_____
_____
_____
_____
_____

Discuss these fears with your partner and work together to find a time that works for you both, knowing it will cost each of you. If you find that your anxiety over this meeting is crippling, it may be an indication that a professional could help, at least in the beginning. Scheduling an appointment with a couple's counselor is nothing to be ashamed of, having an impartial view could help you and your partner communicate in healthier ways and may be more efficient for you.

Overextending Yourself

Yes, yes, yes. Do you feel like you have to tell everyone "yes", while telling yourself "no"? Do you feel the pressures to be the perfect spouse/partner, perfect parent, perfect neighbor, perfect friend, perfect employee?

I hope it is not a newsflash to you that there are only 24 hours in each day; and you are supposed to sleep 8 of those hours. You cannot be perfect (yes, I said it). You cannot do it all. You cannot be everything to everyone. One message I hope you heard in this book is that having healthy expectations and boundaries of other people in your life is crucial to finding anything that resembles balance in your life.

> Your partner can pick up the kids.
> Your kids can do chores.
> Your boss, co-workers, and/or clients can wait.
> Your friends can be empathetic and flexible.
> Your neighbors can help you.
> Your laundry can be done tomorrow.
> Your needs can be prioritized.

Which of those statements stands out to you the most? Why?

_____
_____
_____
_____
_____
_____
_____
_____

I want you to feel confident in your ability to find patience after a long day of working/housework/worrying, etc. to be present with your family. I want you to find patience with yourself so that the to-do list can take a back-seat sometimes to your own desires. If you want to be able to help with homework and spend time being silly with your kids, you will need to use acceptance skills because other things will have to wait. If you want to be present with your partner and to be able to fully engage intimately with them, you can't always save the leftovers for them.

A part of not overextending yourself is realizing that perfection is a farse, a mirage, a delusion. It isn't real. Social media shows you everyone else's "highlight reel" and you are comparing it to your own hidden "bloopers reel". This is not fair to you, your kids, or your partner! Successful people have messy homes, they learn to stop giving it all at work, and they let themselves schedule mental health days!

What is one thing you could stop doing (or stop doing as "perfectly"), to achieve a healthier balance in your life?
_____
_____
_____
_____
_____
_____
_____
_____

Overcommitment

Yes, yes, yes. This may sound repetitive; that is because your habit of saying "yes" to what everyone else wants from you is pervasive and is probably causing problems with overcommitment, which goes hand-in-hand with the prior section on overextending yourself.

Our culture's fixation on "keeping up with the Jones'" and comparison associated with social media has led to a generation of people who have said yes to mortgages that are too large, car loans that are unnecessary, an unrealistic schedule for their family and kids, and parents that are spread far too thin to be effective.

The easy answer with overcommitment is to learn to say "no" to anything that is extra. I suggest you try a season of detox for yourself and your family before resuming activities that are deemed to be values-based. This might mean taking a hiatus from PTO, declining requests to bake cupcakes for the bake sale, declining invitations to engage in "side hustles", not taking on any additional tasks at work, not adding anything more to your family calendar (such as play dates, outings, or seasonal activities), turning down invitations to birthday parties, etc.

Did the suggestion of a "detox season" cause you to feel anxious?

___

What do you think would happen if you say no to the suggested activities for a few weeks? Is a catastrophe likely?

___

Saying "No"

If you are ready to set healthier boundaries surrounding your time and mental energy, you will need to practice saying "no" more often. Telling another person that you cannot do what they are asking you to do is not mean. Telling them that you do not have the resources to be fully available to them is honest and honors your needs as a person and as a parent.

What are some areas that you would like to say "no" in more often?

___

_____
_____
_____
_____
_____

Dialectical Behavioral Therapy presents a structure for communication that is efficient and effective. The skill is presented as an acronym DEARMAN. DEARMAN outlines for you the necessary components for healthy communication, especially when you are asking for something or saying no to something. DEARMAN increases the likelihood that you will maintain your integrity and be heard by the other person. Explore the equation below:

D – Describe:

State the facts of what the situation is. Do not assume the other person knows what you're referring to. Do not include embellishments or judgments.

("I noticed that _____", or "I understand that you would like me to _____")

E – Express:

Tell them how you feel and/or what your opinions are! Do not assume others can read your mind!

("I feel _____ about that request" or "I feel conflicted because _____", or "due to _____ in my life, I'm feeling _____ about committing to more right now")

A – Assert/Ask:

State what your stance is. Be clear and keep your tone neutral. "Wondering with" can be a good strategy here if you need the terms to change or if you are open to negotiation.

("I cannot do it this week, could you _____ and we could reconnect on it next month?", or "I'm wondering if _____ would be possible", or "I appreciate the offer; however, I do not have the ability to attend")

R – Reinforce:

Tell them why they or your relationship will benefit from accepting your answer. This should not sound like a threat – rather, state the positive consequences of their compliance.

(*"so that_____"*, or *"staying home will allow me to spend quality time with my kids this weekend"*)

Practice saying "no" to the situations you identified using the DEAR structure:

_____
_____
_____
_____
_____
_____
_____
_____
_____
_____
_____
_____
_____
_____
_____

If you notice above, I only gave four steps. Those four steps are the DEAR part of DEARMAN and they tell you <u>what</u> to say; however, they do not tell you <u>how</u> to say it. The "how" is important because you do not want to come off as overly aggressive or overly passive. Having a template for body language, voice tone, and intensity behind your message can be just as important, if not more important than the actual message. The MAN part of the acronym alludes to the fact that there are three things a person needs to consider when they are making or declining a request (this can also be used to structure a difficult conversation). Each of these three objectives has an associated acronym that addresses exactly how to deliver the DEAR sentence(s).

1. Consider your objective. What do you want? What are you trying to achieve? The MAN acronym below will allow you to work on this.

2. Consider your relationship. How do you want the other person to feel about you after the interaction? Remember the theme here –we are working on long-term goals, not short-term urges. Attacking the person verbally or being rude with your response might feel good in the short-term; yet is unlikely to help you achieve long-term goals. The GIVE acronym will allow you to preserve the relationship.

3. Consider self-respect. How do you want to feel about yourself after the interaction? The FAST acronym will encourage you to preserve your own values and self-respect.

Most interactions require a combination of the three presented objectives. It is like a recipe; to determine the rations, it is imperative that you decide which objective is most important, second, and least important in the situation. If someone asks you to do something that is against your values, you may find that you need a heaping serving of self-respect (FAST), a scoop of your objective (MAN) and that the relationship isn't particularly important at all. That combination would allow you to say "no" in a way that you are proud of!

A Closer Look at the How Strategies:

When your objective is number one (you need to say no and there isn't room for discussion), the strategy you will use the most of is MAN. MAN is an acronym that reminds you how to deliver your DEAR message from above.

M – Stay Mindful: Keep the focus on the topic at hand. Resist the urge to "beat around the bush" or to let yourself get distracted by the other person's attempts to derail the conversation.

A – Appear Confident: This is especially difficult when you are anxious or feel shame. Have good eye contact and confident body posture!

N – Negotiate: Remember that you often need to give to get. You may need to accept less than you are comfortable with if the long-term goal is being achieved.

When the relationship is top priority (it often is with family situations), the strategy you will use the most of is called "GIVE". GIVE is an acronym standing for:

G – Be Gentle: This means be gentle with yourself and the other person.

I – Act Interested: Yes. ACT! If the relationship is important, hear them out or express interest in their needs/wants. You don't have to change your stance but hearing them out will protect the relationship.

V – Validate: Validating means that you find the grain of truth about what the other person is saying and say it out loud! This often includes acknowledging their feelings/interpretations. Examples include: "I can see why…" "I can see how passionate you feel about this, or "I think I would feel that way too!"

E – Use an Easy Manner: Be authentically yourself, which may include a sense of humor. Soften up what you say and how you say it.

When the number one objective is self-respect, the strategy is FAST. FAST is an acronym that stands for:

F – Be Fair: Be fair to your needs and the other person's needs.

A – No Apologies: Do not be overly apologetic! We all tend to overuse "I'm sorry" as a sentence starter. I suggest you use DEAR and then add a "thank you" when they answer. (If they say no, you could say, "Thank you for considering/taking time to hear me out").

S – Stick to Your Values: This requires you to evaluate your values and know what they are! Don't do things that make you feel immoral. You can even say "I value honesty, so…" or "I value hard work, which is why this is important to me."

T – Be Truthful: Tell the truth; do not act helpless or manipulative.

Once you evaluate your scenario, applying the MAN, GIVE, or FAST recipe will allow you to be confident in your message delivery. Sometimes it will be 90% MAN, 5% GIVE, and 5% FAST (such as interacting with a used car salesman you are unlikely to see again), sometimes it will be 20% MAN, 60% GIVE, and 20% FAST (such as asking your grandma to make a pie for you) or you may see a situation that is 10% MAN, 10% GIVE, and 80% FAST (such as asking your sibling to not drink around you due to your sobriety). The rankings could be different for three different people in the same scenario; you must evaluate your situation in your calmest and most centered state of mind.

Which of the three objectives do you struggle with the most? Why do you think that one is difficult for you?

_____
_____
_____
_____
_____
_____
_____
_____

It is my hope that you can see why overscheduling, overcommitment, and being overly agreeable really are the elephants in the room. We live in a culture where working parents are expected to parent like they don't have a job and work like they don't have kids. This pressure is unreasonable and leads to anxiety, shame, resentment, and depression! It is my desire that the ideas presented in this book allow you to see parenting in a different light and empower you to live a more fulfilling and mindful life.

Showing up for yourself will allow you to feel happier, more fulfilled, passionate, and proud of yourself. This will, in turn, lead to you setting healthier examples for your child(ren) and being able to enjoy parenting!

I am sure it is no surprise that many parents do not really know who they are. The adage "if you don't stand for something, you'll fall for anything" is a helpful saying to remember because if you do not take time to prioritize your values and structure your life accordingly, I believe you will continue to overschedule and overcommit yourself to the demands and desires of other people, leaving less and less of your energy to be available to enjoy both living and parenting. It seems that many families are all stuck ping-ponging from one value to another (such as deciding they value down-time but then regretting it and then deciding they value activity and overscheduling themselves) which prohibits your family from feeling secure in an identity. You must learn the art of balance and consistency, which almost always requires the realization that perfection is unattainable.

As I mentioned in the beginning of this book, you need to know who you are and what you value. You would likely benefit from going back to chapter one and re-doing the values assessment now that you are finished with the book and have a clearer understanding of your needs and why they are important for your relationship with your child(ren). Your values will ebb and flow over time, changing with the seasons of your life. Re-assessing your values can remind you what you would like to keep at the forefront of your mind; this WILL influence your actions. When you get passionate about a topic and educate yourself on that topic, you are more likely to follow-through. That is my hope for you, that you find passion and choose to take action!

Questions to journal on:

1. Are you ready to get creative and problem solve the barriers you found?
2. How would you rate your marital communication and division of labor?
3. Do you need to learn to say "no" to others and say "yes" to yourself?

11 FINAL THOUGHTS

"There is not a right answer; rather, there is a choice that can help you reach your goals more efficiently. – Alexandria Fields

I am a parent and I have worked since the day my girls came into my life. My children were adopted and came to be in my life through the foster care system. I tell you this because at the time of their births and placements with me, I was self-employed and did not get maternity leave. I completely understand the struggle of not having childcare (as children in foster care can only be watched by approved people – it's a lot of paperwork and there are never many options). It is also a reality for our family that our children have special needs as a result of their early life experiences. I tell you this because I, too, know that it can be hard when your kids present with unique challenges. I have had to get very creative over the years to meet my needs.

I am aware that I could stick my kids in front of screens and do what I want. That's not my style. My three children, much to their dismay, do not have tablets/phones. They do not have access to the internet without an adult present. I do things the hard way. I believe it is worth doing the hard work up front and setting them up for more success later in life. I really do understand where you are coming from.

I cannot emphasize enough how much the ideas in this book have enhanced my life, my relationships, and my parenting. It is my hope that you will come away from this book with an increased sense of joy and effectiveness in your life as a working parent. Applying the strategies I shared will not be easy; change requires energy and effort that you may struggle to find at times. I tell you with full confidence though, that applying the ideas shared here may cost you time and energy on the front end but will pay dividends over the coming years of your life!

References

Chapter One:

Linehan, M. (1993). Cognitive-behavioral treatment of borderline personality disorder. New York, New York: The Guilford Press

Linehan, M. (2015). DBT skills training handouts and worksheets (Second ed.). New York, New York: The Guilford Press.

Vanderkam, L. (n.d.). Transcript of "how to gain control of your free time". TED. Retrieved September 27, 2021, from https://www.ted.com/talks/laura_vanderkam_how_to_gain_control_of_your_free_time/transcript?language=en.

Chapter Three:

Seligman, M. E., & Jane., R. K. ; J. L. ; G. (1995). The optimistic child. Boston, Mass.

Chapter Four:

The feeling wheel. The Feeling Wheel | by Gloria Willcox | All The Feelz. (n.d.). Retrieved September 30, 2021, from https://allthefeelz.app/feeling-wheel/.

Imgur. (n.d.). I feel - emotional Word wheel - the Feel wheel - Australian English. Imgur. Retrieved September 30, 2021, from https://imgur.com/tCWChf6.

Carre, S., Mittmann, A., Woodin, E., Tabares, A., & Yoshimoto, D. (2005). Anger Dysregulation, Depressive Symptoms, and Health in Married Women and Men. Nursing Research, 54, 184-192.

Levenson, R., Carstensen, L., & Gottman, J. (1994). Influence of age and gender on affect, physiology, and their interrelations: A study of long-term marriages. Journal of Personality and Social Psychology, 67, 56-68.

Chapter Five:

Cuddy, A. J., Schultz, S. J., & Fosse, N. E. (2018). P-Curving a more comprehensive body of research on POSTURAL Feedback REVEALS Clear evidential value for POWER-POSING EFFECTS: Reply to Simmons and SIMONSOHN (2017). Psychological Science, 29(4), 656–666. https://doi.org/10.1177/0956797617746749

Chapter Six

Yin, Y., Wang, Y., Evans, J. A., & Wang, D. (2019). Quantifying the dynamics of failure across science, startups and security. Nature, 575(7781), 190–194. https://doi.org/10.1038/s41586-019-1725-y

Chapter Seven:

Villa, R. A., & Thousand, J. S. (2000). Restructuring for caring and effective education: piecing the puzzle together. P.H. Brooks Pub.

Sergio Caredda, AboutSergio CareddaDigital Knowmad | Multipotentialite | HR Leader | Transformation Agent | Future of Work thinker | On a mission to re-embed Human into HR. sergiocaredda.eu sergiocaredda, Caredda, A. S., Digital Knowmad | Multipotentialite | HR Leader | Transformation Agent | Future of Work thinker | On a mission to re-embed Human into HR., Sergiocaredda, S., Sergiocaredda.eu, Sergiocaredda, Create Change in Life with a Simple Recipe - The Catalyst Academy Tools, Designing for Change with the Knoster Model - Screenflows.com :: Learn UX to Grow Business, &. (2020, October 10). Models: The Lippitt-Knoster Model for Managing Complex Change. Sergio Caredda. https://sergiocaredda.eu/organisation/tools/models-the-lippitt-knoster-model-for-managing-complex-change/#The_Lippitt-Knoster_Model_for_Managing_Complex_Clippethange.

Pryor, K. (2019). Don't shoot the dog: the art of teaching and training. Simon & Schuster Paperbacks.

Chapter Nine:

Linehan, M. (1993). Cognitive-behavioral treatment of borderline personality disorder. New York, New York: The Guilford Press

Linehan, M. (2015). DBT skills training handouts and worksheets (Second ed.). New York, New York: The Guilford Press.

Sources used throughout the book:

Linehan, M. (1993). Cognitive-behavioral treatment of borderline personality disorder. New York, New York: The Guilford Press

Linehan, M. (2015). DBT skills training handouts and worksheets (Second ed.). New York, New York: The Guilford Press.

Xplore. (n.d.). Inspirational quotes AT BRAINYQUOTE. BrainyQuote. Retrieved September 30, 2021, from https://www.brainyquote.com/.

Fields, A. (2020). Adulting Well: Utilizing the Theories and Strategies of Dialectical Behavioral Therapy. Your Mental Restoration.

ABOUT THE AUTHOR

    Alyx Fields is a mental health therapist specializing in Dialectical Behavioral Therapy from Cincinnati, Ohio. She received her master's degree in social work from the University of Kentucky. She would never preach something that she does not practice! She is a parent of three beautiful girls, a spouse, an adult child, a citizen, an outdoor enthusiast, an artist, a blogger, and a therapist. She does not profess to be a picture of mental perfection as she does not believe that exists. Hypothetically speaking, the Suzy Sunshine's of the world likely have more baggage to unpack than the Debbie Downers. She strives to be a Normal Nancy.

www.ingramcontent.com/pod-product-compliance
Lightning Source LLC
Chambersburg PA
CBHW070937180426
43192CB00039B/2308